TABLE OF CONTENTS

experiences that are most relevant for the jobs you want. Summarize those experiences into a few sentences.

N is for NEXT:

Tell the interviewer the type of experience you'd like next. Your answer should be directly related to the role they're trying to fill. Below are examples for the N section of the P-E-N framework.

Our accountant might say, "Next, I'm looking for a job where I can apply my passion for organizing things. I'd like to work for your accounting firm, where I can build my skills in bookkeeping, auditing, and tax accounting."

Our aspiring consultant could end with, "Next, I want to find a job that will help me accomplish my goal of becoming a more effective business consultant. I've researched my options, and I believe your company is the best fit for my skills and interests. Hopefully, you'll see that I'm a great choice for what you're looking for."

Read on for more on how to land that dream job in your next amazon interview.

CHAPTER 1

SUBMITTING YOUR APPLICATION

Submitting an online application for an open position advertised on www.amazon.jobs —the official recruitment website for the company—is the most commonly used and widely recommended method of getting an interview at Amazon.

You can search for a position of interest through a simple and easy to use search function on the website. The results can be filtered by location, business/job category, or keywords of your choice.

Once you find the position you want to apply for, you need to register a candidate profile on the website, submit your application, and your curriculum vitae (CV).

The recruiters of Amazon receive thousands of applications for advertised positions from all over the world. Therefore, your application and CV should be precise, be able to scan at a glance, and determine your eligibility for the job.

Knowledge and Skill Assessments

Since the beginning of the company, Amazon has always been well-known as a company that recognizes and rewards knowledge and skills of their employees.

They raise the bar of performance with every hire they do, making sure they recruit no one but the best candidate for any given position within the company. In the Amazon hire screening process, the online assessment candidates must complete with their application hold great importance.

There are two different kinds of assessments you may have to face depending on the position you are applying for.

Work Style Assessment

This assessment focuses on the company culture and the leadership principles Amazon employees use at work, and upon which every candidate will be evaluated on.

When answering these assessment questions, candidates are expected to consider the way they have applied the leadership principles in their previous positions. It is to evaluate whether your personality and style of work match the way the company operates.

Work Sample Simulation

These questions are specific to the position you apply for and will evaluate your decision-making skills in different scenarios you may potentially face in that position. It can take anywhere from 20 minutes to 1 hour to complete this assessment.

These assessments are an important step of the initial screening process, and, therefore, often come with a deadline to complete. Many of these assessments are timed and have a specific time duration for completing. It is the first opportunity you have to distinguish yourself from the other applicants with similar educational qualifications and work experience as you, and, therefore, it is crucial to properly answer these questions so as to get the coveted call from the recruiter scheduling the next part of your screening process.

Phone Interview

Applicants who made it through the initial screening proceed to have a phone interview with a recruiter. This interview focuses mostly on the behavioral aspects based on past experience of the candidate. The questions may cover areas such as the challenges you may have faced in a similar position and how you overcame them, the times you took the lead on a project and made it into a success, and the ways you leverage data into strategy.

When you answer these questions, it is important you understand the "data-driven" nature of the company, and relate your own experiences to the leadership principles of Amazon upon which your answers will eventually be evaluated on.

Keep yourself calm and collected when you answer the questions, without panicking or trying to say too much in too little time. Have your CV ready with you to answer any specific questions you may be asked about past experiences. Properly structure your answers and speak confidently.

In-Person Interview / On-Site Visit

If you have made it to this stage, you should have a healthy level of confidence about your eligibility for this position. However, it is also important not to be overconfident due to the high level of demand any job position Amazon has.

During your face-to-face interview, you will likely meet with a panel of interviewers that could range from 2 to 7 people, including a mix of hiring managers, team leads, and other key stakeholders related to your position.

You can wear comfortable and casual clothing since Amazon is a "peculiar" company that does not focus on the way a candidate dresses, but rather on the value they bring to the team.

An in-person interview may last up to an hour depending on the position you applied for. Amazon emphasizes they do not ask "tricky" questions of their potential candidates. Therefore, as long as you have thorough knowledge and practical experience in your area of expertise, you will be able to successfully get through this stage.

If you applied for a technical position such as software development, you need to be able to clearly and analytically discuss technical topics. There will be plenty of behavior questions similar to the phone interview as well. Ultimately, all your answers will be evaluated by the interviewers according to Amazon's leadership principles to make the decision of whether you are fit to be an Amazonian!

CHAPTER 2

QUESTIONS IN THE MANAGEMENT AND LEADERSHIP SPHERE

One example of a question within this sphere is: "Tell me about a time when you were in a leadership position, and you and your group encountered a difficult situation, and how you were able to conquer that hurdle."

A possible scenario that you may have dealt with, and the way to phrase it follows: "When I was still taking my masters, one of our projects was to examine a case, break it down and analyze it, and give a formal presentation to our class and professor. My group chose me to head this project, as they trusted that I would be able to keep the project on track as well as effectively lead the presentation. At the beginning of the project, everything was running smoothly, and we were able to efficiently pinpoint the key issues that the business in question had to handle. However, as we got further along in our analysis, arguments started to flare up between some people in the group, as we were not able to come to a consensus on what the best solutions for the said issues would be. The situation was exacerbated by the fact that we were already tired and stressed and it seemed like we were going nowhere fast. As team leader and head of the project, I took control of the situation by designing a situation that allowed people to compromise, incorporating the ideas of each of the members. Once I presented it to them, I made sure that each and every member agreed with the said compromise, and if they didn't, I tried to find out what their issues about it were. Using this method, I was able to minimize the problems and deal with them effectively, while taking into account all sides. At the end of the day, we were able to present the project on time, and our professor gave us a high grade. I learned much from the experience, but to summarize it on two points: first, the leader must make sure that their team meets their deadlines for their deliverables, and second, that taking people's opinions into account and getting them invested in the success of the project is key to moving forward with ease and reducing interpersonal problems.

Examples Of Questions About Difficult Situations:

One of the questions that's very likely to be asked, as almost everyone can relate to it, and falls under the umbrella of this category is: "Tell me about a time when you had a boss who was difficult to deal with."

An example of a story that you can tell is: "In my last place of employment, which I spent three years in, I had a supervisor who was very difficult to deal with, as he tended to be vague and indecisive. The first couple of months that I spent under his supervision were a struggle for me, so I decided to take the initiative to solve the problem. I scheduled a meeting with him, where I brought up the issues, telling him that I found it difficult to work under him, as he had a tendency to change what he wanted me to do at the very last minute. I even cited examples when I spent a lot of my time working on something, and after a lot of progress was made, he changed the parameters. He was surprised by my straightforwardness, but as I brought it up in a professional manner, and as I was able to give specific examples as to what could have been done if the wasted time had been minimized, he took what I said in consideration. In fact, I felt that his respect increased, and after we had that meeting, his tendency to change his mind at the last minute went away. I learned that it's always to base your arguments on facts, especially when it comes to sensitive issues, and conflict resolution can benefit both of the ones involved, as long as you are able to take the other's perspective into account."

Examples Of Some Of Your Mistakes Or Failures Over The Years

One of the ways this question will be phrased is: "What do you consider to be your biggest failure, and what lessons did you take away from that experience?"

When you answer this question, talk about experiences that show your ability to recover. One example of an answer would be: "During my freshman year in college, I tried to found a campus organization. The organization was supposed to be one that would help Chinese students settle in properly, as there may be difficulties in adjusting to the United States. However, it never really got off the ground, but I was able to discover for myself just what it would take in order to initiate something, and to keep the momentum going. Looking back, I realized that I wasn't able to plan properly and thoroughly, and I ended up rushing things. However, I was able to use the lessons learned from that experience to found a consultation club that allowed business students to gather and discuss cases and trends in the business world. We were able to reach three hundred active members within a year, and we continued growing and developing the club, eventually going beyond our original mission, and I hear the club is still thriving today."

What Are Some Examples Of Your Success?

This question is most often phrased towards what you consider your biggest success. The best way to answer this is to state what you achieved, how you did it, and what you learned from it that contributes to further successes. For example: "The most successful thing that I've done so far in my career is to build a startup from scratch into a business valued at over $6 million. I think the key to achieving that was to develop a clear and strategic overall plan that covered the first few years of the business, then breaking that plan down into more manageable chunks of time governing monthly and quarterly benchmarks. I began to execute the plan while being sure to maintain flexibility in order to adapt to any changes that came along. That experience taught me the importance of planning and flexibility, as well as just how crucial discipline is in order to achieve your end goal."

Examples Of Being Able To Work With Others

Questions about teamwork can vary, but one question often asked, and a question many have problems answering is: "Just how exactly would you deal with a difficult colleague?" When answering, show that you can be firm while remaining understanding of the other person's viewpoint and feelings. An example scenario would be: "When I was in college, I was part of the editorial team of our newspaper. While most of us got along fairly well, there was a team member who was generally abrasive. When I talked about a developing story, he tended to comment sarcastically. He also enjoyed nitpicking and finding problems wherever he could. His difficult behavior led to some missed deadlines and lower productivity. I decided to confront him, and talked to him about how his behavior negatively affected people. He started to go on the defensive, but I calmly gave him examples of his negativity, and explained that constructive criticism should be given in a different manner, if that was his goal. He eventually came to understand, and while he still gave scathing comments every now and again, for the most part, when he criticized others' work, he phrased it in a more civil, constructive manner. I learned that the best way to deal with issues like this is to find overlapping purposes, and propose steps that people can take in order to solve the problem."

Prepare Smart: Prep Fifteen Stories And Practice Spinning Them.

The best way to prepare is to have contingencies. For each of the five major categories that we discussed, it would be good to have at least three stories relating to each of them, for a total of fifteen.

Integrate the Fourteen Main Principles of Amazon in your stories.

Whenever you develop your stories, keep the fourteen principles of Amazon in mind. This allows you to show the interviewer that you're a likely fit for the company. If you're not able to cover all the principles in your fifteen main stories, it may be a good idea to formulate stories that would complete that list.

Questions for Practice and Guidance: Leading and Managing Others

1. Describe a time when you made an unpopular decision and put it into practice.

2. Tell me about a situation where you had to motivate your colleagues.

3. Talk about a time when you demonstrated initiative.

4. Describe a time when you gave a presentation to people who didn't agree with your views.

5. Talk about a situation wherein you needed to be able to sell an idea to someone else.

6. Describe your experiences in building teams.

Questions for Practice and Guidance: Difficult Situations

1. Describe the most difficult situation you've been in and were able to overcome.

2. When was the last time you didn't meet your deadlines?

3. What happened when there was a major change in your job? Were you able to adapt?

4. How would you deal with changing priorities?

5. Describe a situation where you have to make a decision with insufficient knowledge.

6. Tell me what you would do when you're swamped with data and too little time to parse it.

7. What happened the last time that you handled a

risky scenario?

Questions for Practice and Guidance: Past Failures and Mistakes

1. What happened the last time you slipped up?

2. Talk to me about a time where you fell short of your goal.

3. What happened the last time you didn't analyze a scenario properly?

4. Have you ever been disappointed with yourself? Why?

5. Has there been a time when you weren't able to juggle all your responsibilities?

Questions for Practice and Guidance: Successes in Your Career

1. What accomplishment are you most proud of?

2. When's the last time you achieved something you felt was important?

3. What was the best thing you learned from a non-work related incident?

4. Have you ever gone beyond what was expected?

Tell me about that time.

5. Were you ever able to defuse a problem before it escalated?

6. What would you say was your greatest innovation?

7. What was your most creative solution to a problem that came up?

Questions for Practice and Guidance: Working with Others

1. Can you give an example where you had to work with another team?

2. When was the last time you had a disagreement with a co-worker? What happened?

3. Have you ever been a mentor to someone at work? How did it turn out?

4. Have you ever been made to do something which you felt uncomfortable with?

5. When was the last time you compromised? How did it turn out?

6. Tell me about the last time you were able to resolve a conflict.

7. When was the last time you had a negative

interaction with a colleague? What happened?

Questions for Practice and Guidance: Project Manager-Oriented

1. What methods do you use when creating product roadmaps and developing overall strategy?

2. How do you lead those under you?

3. How do you deal with problematic employees?

4. Do you have experience in executing plans that lead to top line results?

5. How often do you take initiative?

6. Are you able to make snap decisions when needed?

7. How adept are you at parsing large data sets?

8. How good are you at gaining consensus?

9. Are you able to adjust for unexpected issues?

10. Are you able to handle working on multiple projects?

11. Have you ever managed a product throughout its entire lifecycle?

Questions Regarding Corporate Culture

Do you remember the discussion on the Strength, Motivation, and Fitness framework? This particular set of questions allows them to judge whether or not you'll be compatible with the corporate culture and values of the company. After all, they want to make sure that you'll fit in, and not cause problems. While many of these should already have been covered by now, there are some aspects that may have been missed, and this is to ensure that you prepare for as much as you can.

Sample Question: What do you do in your free time?

"In my free time, I love to read books. I 'm currently reading a book called "Play Bigger. The book discusses how some of the fastest growing companies are category creators. They taught customers a new way of doing things. The book outlines something known as "Category Creation Strategy" by learning and summarizing from the best category creators of this world — the likes of Facebook, Uber among others."

"I am an avid reader and spend most of my free time with my nose buried in a book. Right now, the book that I am currently reading is called "Play Bigger". This book talks about the characteristics of some of the most rapidly growing corporations in the world today. Some of the companies that have the most rapid growth are known as category creators, who brought in a new paradigm, and taught people an entirely new way of getting things done. The book talks about "Category Creation Strategy", something drawn from the experience and strategies of some of the biggest cutting-edge companies in the world today, like Facebook and Uber."

CHAPTER 3

INTERVIEWING

That is completely natural!

Job interviews are like first dates—good impressions count, awkward moments may occur, and you can rarely predict the outcome until you finally go through with it.

Ultimately it is about being yourself, staying calm, letting your personality shine, and making sure you communicate well as to why you are a good candidate for the position!

According to a recruiter from Amazon, they always treat their potential candidates as customers, making sure their interview experience is comfortable and delightful. You do not need to worry about interviewers intentionally making you feel uncomfortable, which is an old school interviewing method not practiced by many companies nowadays, including Amazon.

Another important thing to remember when you face your interview is that Amazon has the need to hire you as much as you need to be hired by Amazon. They have thousands of positions to fill constantly, and are cheering you on to perform your best so they can make you a part of their team. They are not there to watch you fail. Do not treat the situation like they are doing you a favor by calling you for an interview. Own your expertise and confidently face them.

Behavioral Interviewing Overview

Amazon has a behavioral approach to their interviews, which is one of the most effective and popular interview techniques widely practiced today. To put it simply, in a behavioral interview, the recruiter assesses a candidate's skills and performance by asking questions based on their past behavior.

To successfully answer during a behavioral interview, you should have clear and analytical knowledge of your industry and your past work. It is not just about remembering the responsibilities of your past jobs, but more about being able to speak of them in a way that you can fully explain your contribution to them.

Go through your performance reviews from previous jobs to get an outsider's perspective on the way you work. Brainstorm answers to all the possible questions you might get according to your job description.

The Philosophy & Questions

Amazon is a customer-centric, data-driven company that hires people with exceptional leadership skills. Every answer you give during your interview should be grounded on these facts.

Show your interviewers that not only are you a good candidate for the position, but would also be a great addition to Amazon's team of employees, be a valuable asset which understands and upholds their precious company values.

Tell me about yourself.

This simple question usually breaks the ice at the beginning of the interview. It is perhaps the most important question you get since you will not only make your first impression, but also set ground for the rest of the interview. You don't want to drag this on too much, nor do you want to sound like you do not have much to say about yourself.

At this point of the interview, your interviewers are rooting for you to be successful. They are giving you the chance to lead and set the tone for the next questions. What you should not do now, is repeat your resume.

That is redundant and waste time of you and your interviewer.

This is your 60-second sell—your elevator pitch. Concisely and coherently summarize your professional background. It is fine to add a little fun detail about yourself to lighten the mood and perhaps get a laugh, but do not overdo it.

Highlight your expertise, your experience, your special training or qualifications. End with your enthusiasm to join this company and the e-commerce industry you are going to get in to.

Why do you want to work for our company?

Amazon is a company made with passion and a great level of innovation. Talk about your experience, expertise, and how you can practically apply them within the company.

What strengths do you bring to the team?

Amazon always aims for exceptional workers who will move up the ladder quickly as the company expands. The skills and strengths they are looking for should be unique and be in line with their leadership principles.

Use your knowledge of the leadership principles and relate them to your own strengths when you answer this question. For example, connect your tendency to pay great attention to detail with customer obsession and ensuring every single aspect of a project is done to perfection before it reaches the end customer.

Play up your sense of urgency and great teamwork skills. Show them you have done your research on the company. Show you are aware of the kind of employee they are looking for and you have what it takes to be that.

What is the salary you are expecting?

Amazon recruiters do not ask their prospective hires their salary history. When you prepare your answer to this question, you do not need to base it on the salary you are already getting. Do your research on the average salary people of your position get according to which state/country you are in, and make it clear you are open to offers as well.

CHAPTER 4

QUESTIONS TO THROW YOU OFF

Especially when it comes to newer millennial workplaces, your interviewer might throw some fun and quirky questions in. This is usually just going to be an attempt at trying to understand who you are without directly asking you.

Employers often want to get your sense of humor. It's crucial that you are professional, but not every position will require a stiff suit and a straight face. Questions like these are to see how you might react in a casually professional scenario.

They want to throw you off in an attempt to get the most realistic response from you. These aren't trick questions! There's no perfect response. It's simply a way to gauge what you might actually be like outside of a professional setting.

"Are you willing to relocate for this position?"

This is a question that you might not get asked if you are interviewing for a more entry-level position. They still might slip it in there just to see how you react. It can give them a little bit of insight into how dedicated you are to the position. No matter what you might be willing to do, this is a suitable answer:

"I am always interested in exploring new avenues and would definitely consider any opportunity for advancement whether it's professional or personal."

"What is the last book, movie, and television show that you watched? What is the last video you watched on YouTube?"

This is a question based on your personality and on wanting to get to know more about you. NEVER lie to make yourself sound smarter. It might be tempting to say that you just watched that recently released 3-hour economics documentary, but the person conducting the interview might have just watched that last night and is ready to talk about it in great detail! Ensure that you are being truthful and let your personality shine through. They will get a good sense of who you are and the things you like when you honestly share media that interests you. Who knows what you might legitimately be able to connect with someone on! Never say that you haven't read a book in a while either. Before going into the interview, even if it's something that is totally unrelated to books or TV, have an answer for this one prepared.

"If you had unlimited time and money right now, where would you go on vacation?"

Where a person would like to travel to can be a really interesting topic. You might be able to discuss what this place is actually like with them as well, if they'd been there themselves. Have a reason that you want to go there too, don't just say something like Paris or Tokyo just because they're popular destination spots. It will make you look better if you show true passion about this answer.

"What type of animal would you be?"

This is something commonly asked. What the person conducting the interview is hoping to gain is just a little insight as to how you think of yourself. Not only this, but they are also curious what qualities you might have that you hadn't discussed yet. Don't pick the obvious dog or cat, but if you really must, elaborate on what interesting qualities they have that you believe you do too. Pick something a little unexpected. Here's a fun answer that can work, but don't repeat it verbatim of course!

"I would have to say that I would want to be some sort

of tropical bird. I would like the ability to fly above everything else and have that view, while also being familiar with tropical waters as well. I certainly wouldn't want to be a bird that gets hunted, though! I'd just like to be a part of the beautiful world and experience all that there is."

"What is your biggest pet peeve? What little habit do other people do that drives you crazy?"

This is a little insight into what it is that might make you tick. It's a human answer that gives the person conducting the interview something to really understand you. Do you hate people that tap their feet? Does it bug you when someone sneezes without covering their mouth? Many things are commonly hated, but what might yours be that's a little different than everyone else's? Have your answer be unique enough to stand out but not negative to the point where you are generally insulting multiple different people.

"Let's say you go out to dinner somewhere nice and order a delicious meal on the menu. Then, when the food comes out, it's the completely wrong order. How would you handle this situation?"

This is a great way to get an idea of how you might handle situations that aren't always ideal. Are you someone that is passive and is just going to go with the flow? Are you more likely to speak up and tell the truth if that's what the situation is calling for? This question will let the person conducting the interview know how you can handle unexpected turns and how you might be able to approach a situation that makes you uncomfortable.

"Are you comfortable listening to orders from someone that is younger than you, or has less educational or work experience? Are you comfortable delegating tasks to those that are older than you, or that have a much higher level of experience?"

Surprisingly, this can be an issue that many people have. Some older individuals don't want to take orders from those who are younger than them. Those who are younger might sometimes have trouble giving direction to those that are older. It's important to remember that experience doesn't always equate to age. The best answer would be "yes," but always ensure that you are providing a "why" as well. Remember that you don't have to tell them your age, simply share the truth about how you might feel in that scenario.

"If you won the lottery right now, what would be the one of the first few things you would do with the money?"

We all have dreams of winning the lottery or getting that letter from an anonymous relative telling us they left us the inheritance! While this is a common dream that we have, what is different is what we would all decide to do with the money if we were ever to actually come across a large sum like that! What you choose to say will reveal the truth about your personality. Don't make it too professional by saying that you would "save it all." Think of something creative to spend it on that shows the person conducting the interview you have a fun and impulsive side.

"What would your superpower be if you had the choice?"

This is a fun one to discuss as well. Questions like these can really break up the tension and keep the interview flowing naturally. Depending on what they ask, have a few different answers. Something like invisibility or telekinesis is common and could be applied to the job. You might also want to consider what power those who know you might give to you depending on your personality. Maybe your friends and family would say that you are someone who is a superhero of solving problems or making everyone laugh. Cater this to your personality and keep the job in mind as well.

"If you could meet anyone dead or alive, whom would you pick?"

This is a popular question that we often hear discussed outside of just the context of professional interviews. Make sure that you have an idea prepared for what you want to say. Be honest and don't just go for someone obvious. It can be easy to want to say, "Jesus," or a past president or another strong figure. These are good answers! But they are also answers others are likely to give. Switch it up and say someone that you would genuinely be interested in meeting and having a conversation with. Always remember to provide the "why" for this as well.

"What professional sport would you play? What position do you think you'd thrive in?"

Not all of us are athletic, but that doesn't mean we can't still think about what kind of sports we would be best at. This is a fun question that will give the person conducting the interview an idea of what your personality is like. Would you be good at something more relaxed like golf? Are you instead a person who would be best at wrestling? Pick something based on your skills, what you are passionate about, and based around what the job might be.

"What is your all-time favorite game? Whether it's a board game, video game, or sport, what is your favorite?"

Sometimes people will refer to life just as one big game. The game looks different for everyone, however, some of us prefer logic games, others would like to be able to win with their sheer physical strength. The type of games that people like to play, and which ones they're good at, can reveal a lot about their personality. State honestly what your favorite game is, no matter what it might be. Provide a "why" as well. Do you enjoy sitting down and being strategic? Are you someone that enjoys friendly conversation? Share with them what kinds of games bring you the most joy, and which ones you always seem to win as well.

"Do you like to sing in the shower?"

This question seems weird, especially since they're

asking about what you do in the shower! The point of this question is often to find out your confidence level. Most of us sing in the shower, but some might say a bashful, "no" as their cheeks turn rosy when asked the truth. Be yourself! If you do sing in the shower and aren't afraid to admit it, have a few ideas of what your favorite songs to sing might be. Here's a fun example of what a good answer would be:

"I love to sing in the shower, but I don't think my roommate appreciates me singing as much! My go-to would be between ABBA and Beyoncé!"

"What is the worst movie of all time?"

This can be a hard one, and something that you might be afraid to answer as well! What if the worst movie you've ever seen is the best one they have ever seen? It's OK to have a simple answer for this one. Maybe you state something like a kid's movie, and your reasoning for it being the worst is because it made you cry! This is just a fun question to better figure out what your personality might be like.

"Who is the funniest person you know?"

You already answered a question about your sense of

humor earlier, but this question gives the person conducting the interview a more practical idea of the kinds of things that you think are funny. You can answer first with a celebrity or stand-up comedian if you want. Don't forget to include people that you actually know, such as your brother or your best friend. Be honest and share reasons why you think they're so funny, and what they do the most that always seems to leave you laughing.

"Where did you meet your closest circle of friends?"

You can find out a lot about a person and really understand who they are by where they met their friends. If your three closest friends are from kindergarten, then it's clear that you are pretty good at keeping relationships healthy in your life. If you have a long list of friends and say that you met some in college, some in high school, some from other jobs, and some from going out, it means that you are a pretty social person! Be honest with this as well! If you don't have a lot of friends, you don't have to say that. You can phrase it by stating:

"Most of my friends I've had for a really long time so it's

hard to remember exactly where we met. I like to keep a few close friends that I know are reliable and fun to be around instead of having many friends that I might not be as close with."

"If you had one wish right now, what would you wish for?"

This is a great question and can reveal just how quickly someone can think on their feet. The most common answer would be to wish for "unlimited wishes". That is also a common wish, however, so don't be afraid to get creative. Maybe you wish for a credit card with an unlimited amount of money on it. Perhaps you wish that you could directly pick who the next president is. Maybe you wish for all your friends and family to live happy lives. Whatever it is, try to go with the first thing that comes to your mind when the question is asked, as long as it is reasonable and professional of course!

What is your least favorite chore to do?

This is a great question that can really reveal a lot about a person. Some people might state that their least favorite chore is to sweep. Others would say that putting away laundry is their least favorite. These are all common chores that we all have to do, whether you are someone interviewing to be the CEO or if you want the entry-level position at your local fast food chain. Well of course, some people will have maids if they are that wealthy, but still, answer honestly and discuss with the person conducting the interview why it is that you hate that specific chore.

"Let's say you are walking down the street after this interview and you find a stray dog. What would your plan be to take care of the situation?"

This is a great question that can reveal a lot about your character. Are you bold enough to take matters into your own hands and find a happy solution? Would you walk away and let this dog fend for itself? Obviously, we wouldn't say that we'd just leave it, but the interviewer would still be able to pick up on how much of the truth you are telling. Honestly think about what you would do and tell them in a way that is truthful and organized. This question might be presented in a few different ways as well, some maybe asking, "What would you do if you found a wallet on the street," and so on.

"What is a secret that you don't want your coworkers to know? What is something that you

purposely kept off your resume?"

This is a hard question, maybe one of the most challenging ones that you will come across! You don't want others to know, so that's the whole point of keeping it a secret. It is still a way to catch you off guard and get you out of your comfort zone. Think of this one before you go into the interview. Don't lie of course, but you also don't need to reveal your absolute deepest darkest secret. Here's an example of what you might say:

"I probably wouldn't want anyone to know that I got an award five years ago for eating 50 hot dogs in less than 10 minutes. I was proud at the time, but not something I want to be known for at this new job!"

CHAPTER 5

QUESTIONS TO EXPECT

Some employers like to scour resumes and applications rather than focus on how an applicant's experience benefits the employer. You may have an interviewer who goes chronologically through your resume and quizzes you at length about your daily responsibilities at each job. This employer is more concerned with the "what" than the "how". Do you really want to work for someone like that? If so, just answer all the interviewer's questions honestly and forthrightly while trying to pepper your responses with examples of how you were able to do the "what" with creative "how".

Other employers, though, want to understand how your work and life experiences can help move the company's mission forward. They may ask more questions related to how you've learned skills and how you incorporate them into your everyday work.

Just about every interviewer asks the same or very similar questions. Here are some you should be prepared to answer. There are a variety of categories into which interview questions fall, but there are also different types of questions. More often, employers are using "Behavioral Questions" to help them understand how you would behave in a particular situation. (Have you heard the saying that "Past behavior is the best predictor of future performance"? It's true!)

OPENING or ICE-BREAKER QUESTIONS

Tell me about yourself OR Why do you think you'd be a good fit for this position? This is a good place for your Elevator speech, jazzed up with a little more information and a smooth segue into why you'd be a good fit for the employer's opening. A little about me: I currently work at Baker and Sharp as an Accounting Associate; I've been there three years. I graduated from Tulane University with a Bachelor's in Accounting before accepting the position with Baker, and was able to maintain a 3.9 GPA throughout college while working part-time for a small tax accounting firm. At Baker, I've been working with 8 to 10 of their smaller clients, reviewing their books each month, doing Journal Entries, and any other accounting tasks that need to be done like maintaining their Charts of Account, General Ledgers, recording and depreciating Assets, maintaining balance sheets and income statements. I'm ready to move into a more responsible role but nothing's available at Baker so I'm looking outside. Your ad for a Financial Analyst sounds ideal. I have several years of experience using Hyperion and SAP, and I'm really looking for something I can sink my teeth into. And Palmer Associates is a bit larger than Baker and Sharp, so I believe I may have more room for future growth here. Can you tell me a little more about the role you have available?

OR

I started out at Jamison Brothers in Counter Sales in 2004 and worked my way up to Associate Marketing Manager three years ago. I finished my MBA this past June and I'm looking for a Marketing Manager role now in a larger organization. Jamison's been wonderful; it's been a great learning experience. I'm ready now to tap into all those years of knowledge along with my MBA and move into a more responsible role. When I saw your ad for an Online Marketing Manager, I thought the role sounded ideal – it really matches my skills and passions. And of course the Pettibone Agency is such a well-known and respected firm, such an iconic brand. I'd love to hear more about what you're looking for in an Online

Marketing Manager.

For the Good Fit question: My experience and education dovetail perfectly with your job requirements, and I believe I have some unique qualifications that set me apart from others that you'll find useful. In addition to experience using standard Accounting software packages, I have experience in programming and my Excel skills are Expert level.

How did you learn about this position? OR Why did you apply for this position? The interviewer wants to make sure you've bothered to actually read the job description Enthusiastic response: I spotted it on Monster and it really struck a chord with me because the ad describes my skillset so perfectly, yet there are still many challenges still to be conquered. BONUS POINTS if you've printed and brought the job ad with you to the interview, complete with tiny notations.

What's your work philosophy? The interviewer wants to know that you operate by a set of standards, and whether those standards fit with the company's standards. My work philosophy is the same as my personal philosophy. I believe that we're all here for a purpose and we need to be partners in every way. If my job is to identify and hire employees who fit the culture and believe in the mission of the organization, then it's incumbent on me to fulfill that aspect of my job to the best of my ability every day, while making sure my efforts support every other employee's needs as well.

What was your Overall GPA at the time you graduated? The interviewer is interested in finding out how you performed in school. S/he may even ask what your GPA was in your Major. The reason interviewers find this question important is because it shows how hard you worked and how seriously you took getting your degree. If your GPA was 2.6, there's no sugar-coating it. Don't try to add decimal places ("It was 2.677 but if it weren't for that one Statistics class that was super-tough, it would have been 3.0") My Overall GPA was 3.6; my Major GPA was 3.8. BONUS POINTS for graduating with honors.

EDUCATION and CREDENTIAL QUESTIONS

Why did you decide to go into Biomedical Engineering?" The interviewer is trying to find out whether your career choice was a deliberate act or if you simply took the easiest classes to get through school as quickly as possible. I've always had a fascination with medicine, but didn't want to be a doctor or nurse. I'd gotten top grades in Math and Science courses, and a High School career counselor suggested I look into Biomedical Engineering. After learning more about the field, I was excited about the idea of using both engineering and medicine to improve people's lives.

Why did you choose Vanderbilt University for your education? Here, the interviewer is interested in your decision making process. They're trying to learn: whether your decision making is thoughtful and deliberate, perhaps the approach you took to reach your decision, whether there were any mitigating circumstances that caused you to choose one school over another? (Boyfriend was going to Vanderbilt; wanted to be with him – not a good answer) Once I knew I wanted to study Biomedical Engineering, I took my career counselor's advice and researched the best schools – both from an academic standpoint and from a personal standpoint. I wanted to get a top-notch, well-rounded education with opportunities for public service, and Vanderbilt has allowed me to achieve all of those goals.

What are you most proud of having achieved in your career so far? Your response should reflect something your interviewer can relate to, not something that's so industry-specific it only applies in the matchbook printing industry, and you're interviewing for a position in management consulting. Broaden your thought process, know this question will come, and be prepared with several possible responses, from which you can select the one most likely to be seen by someone in the job for which you're interviewing. I had the opportunity to become Green Belt Six Sigma Certified in my current role, and the tools and methodologies I learned have enabled me to really shine when it comes to data analysis.

What professional certifications or licenses do you hold? How long have you had them? What are the requirements for maintaining or renewing them? The interviewer wants to make sure you're committed to any professional certifications or licenses you've taken the time to attain. Most certifications or licenses will require that you take exams or classes, or attend seminars to stay current with trends in your industry or specialized expertise area. I'm certified as a Microsoft Certified Solutions Associate (MCSA) and a Microsoft Certified Solutions Expert (MCSE). I get re-certified every three years, and re-certification requires taking an exam. My last recertification exam was in August of last year and my score on the exam was 98%.

EXPERIENCE QUESTIONS

Tell me more about the three Internships you had – what your responsibilities were, and what you took away from the experiences. The Interviewer wants to get a feel for how diligent you were in seeking out Internship opportunities that fit with your career aspirations or that helped form your career decisions. Summers working at the Burger Palace don't count as Internships. My first Internship was as a sophomore. It was with a small medical device manufacturing company and I was fortunate to work within the Research and Development department.

My second Internship was as a junior. I found an opportunity with a large pharmaceutical manufacturer, where I learned how drugs are being added to implants to help the human body accept them better. It was great to actually see how research and pharmaceuticals are improving the patient experience.

For my final Internship, which was just this past Winter break, I was invited back to the medical device manufacturer by my supervisor, Dr. Batap. He really took me under his wing and helped me understand how the design and engineering of a new medical implant device is done. I learned about new materials that are just coming into use, and about some of the older technologies – and why the new materials are so much better.

All in all, I think my Internship experiences were extremely beneficial and helped prepare me well for a long and interesting career with Wilkinson.

Why weren't you promoted at your last job? The employer is concerned that your work was only average, not deserving of promotions. I'm certain that the reason I wasn't promoted is because I didn't have the right credentials at that time. I have, however, completed my degree and together with my years of experience, it's time for me to move on to something for which I'm highly-skilled and trained.

You're a Mechanical Engineer, and technologies are always changing in your field. What are the most significant trends you see in your field of expertise right now? How do you keep current on technology trends in your specialty? The employer wants to make sure you aren't just resting on your college degree, assuming that nothing in the world of Mechanical Engineering has changed since you graduated college 14 years ago. Of course, much has changed, and as a professional, you need to be keeping current with changes. The employer wants to make sure you're keeping current, and the best way to do that is to ask you what resources you use. (If you can't name any, you're in trouble) Every field of science changes so rapidly, it's hard to keep up with it. But I do my best, because I love what I do, and I'm interested in staying relevant. I'm a member of the Mechanical Engineering Society. We receive weekly email news updates with the latest research and trends. In addition, I attend the annual Conference of Mechanical Engineers, which is a week-long program packed with learning and networking opportunities. I also subscribe to Mechanical Engineer's Quarterly, a magazine devoted to the field of Mechanical Engineering, and I'm a Certified Senior Mechanical Engineer, which requires that I get a certain amount of re-training annually to keep my certification current. Some of the training is available online; some of it is only available through classes and seminars. BONUS POINTS if you've written (and had published) articles to professional publications.

Tell me about a time that you worked with data – compiling it, interpreting it, and presenting it. If you are in a non-technical profession, this question is designed to see if you are comfortable with information not directly related to your position. If you are in a technical profession, data collection and analysis should be second-nature. Here's your opportunity to demonstrate your comfort level with the data collection and analysis process. I gather, compile and analyze data every day in my role as a Quality Engineer with Quality Reps. But I'm also interested in the data common to the industry at large, so I collected data on the rate of Quality Returns in the medical equipment industry and prepared some Pareto charts and other analysis to share with my managers.

Why do you want this job? Under no circumstances should you say "because I need a paycheck." Don't even joke about that. You want THIS particular job because you're extremely well-qualified and have had similar experience in the past that would help inform your future career. When I saw the ad for this position, I just knew it was a great fit for my skillset and I believe I'd fit well within the organization. When I did some online research on the company, I found that current and former employees consistently rate you 4 out of 5 stars. That says to me that this is a well-run organization that values its employees. BONUS POINTS: If you've become familiar with some new technology the company is working on and it's your field of expertise, make sure the interviewer knows that.

CHAPTER 6

AFTER THE INTERVIEW

After your interview, you shouldn't just sit around on your hands and wait to hear back from the hiring manager.

Instead, start by being proactive and proving that you want the job. This will increase your likelihood of landing your ideal job.

One way in which you can be proactive is to complete an interview assessment.

To do this, the same day you have an interview and while it is still fresh in your memory, write out a list of what you were asked and your answers.

This will help you to remember in case of follow-up interviews with the company or if you are looking to improve your interview skills. If you wish you had asked questions or mentioned specifics, then write these down as a note.

That way, if you get the opportunity for a follow-up interview, you can remember to speak on the matters next time.

You will have wanted to get the names of everyone involved during the interview process.

Then, you can write out a thank you note to send to the company. This sends a good impression to everyone involved and sends the message that you are a considerate team-player.

Decisions regarding the candidates are often made quickly, but not always.

A certain manager might be swamped with work and unable to quickly contact people to let them know whether or not they got the position.

However, in case the decision is made quickly, you should continue to make a good impression after the interview.

You can do this by sending a follow-up email to the hiring manager either the same day of your interview or the following day.

This can be a short email which thanks the manager for their time, reaffirms that you believe yourself to be an excellent fit and would love to work for the company and ask any questions you might have missed the opportunity for during the interview.

Think beyond your current job opportunity and consider your longer career goals.

One way you can benefit these goals is to reach out to the hiring manager through your professional social media, adding them on either Twitter or LinkedIn.

By building a long-term relationship, you will increase your connections for the future.

Getting a job will require references. However, you don't want these references to be surprised with phone calls out of the blue. Therefore, alert your references, letting them know that they might receive either an email or a phone call. During this time, it is a good idea to softly sell yourself, explaining why the position is a good fit and why you are the right candidate for the job.

Finally, if you get the job, you will need to work on salary negotiations. Not all positions have room for negotiation; they might have a standard starting rate they are unwilling to budge on.

However, ask if you can negotiate your salary because it is a great opportunity if they are willing.

When negotiating for a higher salary, you need to be prepared with:

An ability to prove your case, with specifics on the value

you offer the company.

The knowledge that you will likely face resistance. Be ready to answer questions as to why you deserve an increase in salary.

Be Firm and Flexible. It can be hard to be both of these, but it is important to strike a balance. You don't want to be a pushover, but you also don't want to give up the ideal position because you are unwilling to meet your employer halfway.

In order to negotiate your salary, it is important to objectively know how much you are worth.

Research the starting salary of the position within your state. It is important that when researching this, you know your state specifically, as each state has its own minimum, standard, and high-income wage. When considering this, it is important to take your education, experience, and skills in mind. If the market is saturated with people of similar skill and experience, then you might not have as much of a case.

However, if you have rare experience and skills then you can afford to negotiate more.

If you go to Glassdoor, they have a Know Your Worth calculator, which will help you to understand how much other people in your field are being paid.

This does not take experience and individual skills into account, but it is a good starting place.

Once you have all of this knowledge, you can create a ballpark range in which you would like your starting salary to be. This will help you to be both firm and flexible.

When negotiating, keep these tips in mind:

- Have a salary ballpark range, not a single sum.

- Practice your pitch a few times before your negotiation.

- Don't sell yourself short.

- Be confident in yourself and your delivery.

- Be gracious to your employer.

- Understand your leverage.

- Don't accept the first offer.

If you keep this knowledge in mind, then you should be able to successfully negotiate a salary that works out both for you and your employer.

CHAPTER 7

WHAT TO DO WHILE WAITING

Arrive early

Almost every interview-related book and article will tell you how important punctuality is. You are certainly expected to be on time on the day of the interview. The surest way to avoid tardiness is to arrive at the venue at least 30 minutes ahead of your scheduled interview time. But what will you do with all this time in your hands? Do you spend it nursing the little butterflies fluttering in your stomach?

Use the time productively by observing the reception area

Look for company-related literature, which are likely to contain their annual reports, brochures of their products and services, and their newsletters. Determine the business's flagship product and the recent events that the company took part in. This way, you'll get to stock up on your knowledge of the company or the trade.

Converse with the receptionist

If no such literature is available, and if the receptionist isn't too busy, you can casually squeeze some useful information out of him/her. Greet the receptionist. Introduce yourself and ask for his/her name. Ask him/her how he/she is doing. Too often, applicants regard receptionists as room fixtures, which is a huge mistake because as an inside person, a receptionist can be a valuable ally.

Example:

Applicant: "Hello. I'm _____. I'm scheduled to see Mr./Mrs./Ms. _____ at ____ ."

Receptionist: "Please have a seat..."

Applicant: "Thank you. And your name is..?"

Receptionist: (name)

Applicant: "Hello, (call receptionist by name). How are you doing?"

Receptionist: "I'm fine, thanks."

Applicant: "I have an interview with _____. So, how is he/she today?"

Receptionist: "Oh, well, a bit stressed. You know how it is..."

Applicant: "I see. Anything out of the ordinary?"

Receptionist: "Well, it's just that the annual sales meeting is almost upon us again. Things always get pretty tense during this time of the year."

See how being friendly could make all the difference?

Now you know what your interviewer's current mood is. Now you know what your potential employer's present problem is. This means you can now think of how you'll be able to make him see that you are capable of easing his load.

Example:

"Mr./Mrs./Ms. _____, thank you so much for seeing me. I appreciate your time, especially since I know how busy you are with your sales meetings. I understand completely what that's like."

Now, this is a way to make a grand entrance.

Another advantage of being friendly with the receptionist is that knowing you by name makes it more likely for him/her to prioritize your follow-up call after the interview.

Calm the Butterflies

Even before you enter the interview room, be aware of your body and control all voluntary and involuntary gestures, which may subconsciously communicate fear and nervousness. Nervous body language reveals your lack of confidence. Moreover, the interviewers won't appreciate you making them feel terrible about themselves. After all, you're going to an interview, not into a monster's lair. Stop doing the following:

twirling your hair

licking your lips

biting your nails

swinging your legs

tapping your foot

touching your nose

touching your mouth

wringing your hands

When you allow your body to exhibit any of these outward signs of anxiety, it further convinces your subconscious that you are indeed anxious.

What if your interviewer is late?

The worst thing you can do is to just sit there and well... wait. When you arrive at the venue, make sure that you check in with the receptionist so your interviewer knows that you have arrived.

If there is no receptionist present, then wait until one minute after the exact time. For this reason, you have to make sure that your clock is in sync with the office's clock. Next, walk towards the interviewer's door and knock.

Five minutes after the scheduled time, approach the receptionist and ask if he/she has had any word from the interviewer.

Example: "I'm scheduled for an interview at (exact time). Have you heard from Mr./Ms./Mrs. _____?"

At twenty minutes past the scheduled time, approach the receptionist again and request that he/she check in with your interviewer.

Example: "I wonder if it might be possible for you to check in with Mr./Mrs./Ms. _____ . He/she is quite late."

One hour after the scheduled time, get a piece of paper and a pen (you should be carrying these) from your folder/attaché and then write a note for the interviewer.

Example:

Dear Mr./Mrs./Ms. _____,

It is (state exact time), an hour past the scheduled interview time. This has left me to assume that you have been detained by some unavoidable and unexpected circumstance. Perhaps it would be best if we re-schedule the interview. You may reach me at (your number). I shall check in with you later this afternoon.

Sincerely,

(your name)

Fold the note and then hand it over to the receptionist. Politely ask the receptionist to make certain that the interviewer receives the letter. No matter how you choose to write your letter, make sure that you keep it polite and professional. There must be no hint of anger, disappointment, or annoyance.

What if the interviewer finally does show up?

If this happens, then proceed with the interview and forget everything. It will do you absolutely no good to go into an interview with a chip on your shoulder. Chances are, your interviewer has a perfectly good reason for being late. That said, he is under no obligation to explain the details to you. Moreover, depending on the circumstance, you should reflect too on whether or not it would be fine for you to work for an employer who thinks nothing of keeping his subordinates waiting for him.

CHAPTER 8

FACE TO FACE WITH THE BOSS

Perhaps your interview is actually with the person who would be your direct boss. Rather than looking at this meeting as daunting do your best to view this as a positive as it allows you to get a feel yourself for the dynamic you two would share. When you interview with someone who is not going to be your direct supervisor you miss an opportunity to really get a true feel for how the job will feel, function, and even miss out on asking specific questions of your supervisor which you may otherwise not ask if you are interviewed by an outside party. Take this opportunity as a blessing in disguise and remember the interview is for you to assess the company for you as well as them to you.

Certainly, remain polite and positive. Do your best to smile and make eye contact. Above all be professional. Speaking ill of others or your own past experiences is never a good way to gain brownie points with a potential boss. If the potential supervisor is steering the conversation that direction it would be advisable to ask yourself if working in an environment full of drama and gossip is best suiting for your longevity at a company.

Be sure to ask questions of your potential boss of their experience working with the company and of course their expectations of someone in that position. It would be wise to inquire about the career path set forth for someone taking the position. It is always helpful to gain a little foresight to what you would be working on by finding out what the goals for that position or the company are. This will give you an idea if the goals which are expected to be met are achievable.

Another important question to ask is what success looks like to that potential boss. In asking this you will be able to assess if their idea of success is completely unreasonable or if they are well within the scope of what you have done previously. It would be helpful to you in the future being employed but the company to know prior to the acceptance of the position what types of projects are being pursued and what the expectations for those projects are and your own personal responsibility for each one.

Avoid being afraid or concerned when speaking to your potential boss. Do your best to be confident and remember that they are just a person like you. In any interview it is advised to avoid flashy or revealing clothing. Some people may be sensitive to smells so refrain from wearing strong scents.

Practice your best hygiene and ensure you look your best. You want to make the best first impression possible. Never be late and do your best to arrive to the interview early and prepared with any documents or forms required if any are needed.

How Would Your Colleagues Describe You?

A potential employer will ask this question so they can get an idea of how you see yourself through other's eyes. Are you the type of person to be overly inflated in a self-centered mentality or are you the type of person who is realistic in how the world sees them? Your potential employer is always looking for a clearer picture of your inner workings and asking this question will give them an idea of the picture you paint of the world around you, your point of view for the situations you encounter, and if you are the type of person to only see things from your own point of view or if you are able to use your own discernment.

When responding, focus your response on the positive things they would say about you and bring those responses back to how that aided you when working in a team. Steer clear of painting yourself as someone who is perfect and can do no wrong. In the same respect, refrain from portraying yourself as someone who fails consistently.

In your response avoid speaking of personal situations. It is best to let the past rest and avoid bringing into the conversation any negative experiences or people with whom you have had encounters. Speaking on someone's personal matters as justification for your point of view will make you appear as a gossip and ultimately will cause you to appear as the negative person in the encounter as the other person in question is not there to defend themselves. Do your best to stick to a true and honest opinion of what your colleagues would say about you and your work ethic. Hone in on the most positive aspects of how you work well with others and how you compliment the talents of others.

Also avoid talking about any confrontations you have had in the past. Should the employer desire information regarding an issue which has been brought to your attention they will ask. Bringing attention to conflicts will only serve to make the employer assume you seek out drama. Those who create drama in a workplace slow down processes and ultimately cost the company more money. They are also less likely to remain happy in a position for a long time and can create rifts within the team structure.

How Do You Work Under Pressure?

Employers who ask this question are asking because they have high stress situations and timeline which must be met. Sometimes paid bonuses and overall evaluations of success are dependent on these timelines and goals. Should you be unable to handle stress, and work well with the team in those stressful situations, the company would like to know. Every job has its own versions of stress but when asked this question it is because they would like to know what kind of person you are when faced with deadlines and strict goals.

Positions where specific numbers must be met within a certain time frame will ask this question because numbers are important to any company. If the person responsible for reaching those numbers is unable to work within the parameters of the position, they are not the best candidate for the job. Furthermore, if the person is someone who has difficulty with others, becomes a sloppy worker, mean, unable to follow instructions, or loses their ability to problem solve when they find themselves in a high pressure situation, the employer would like to weed out those potential employees.

Just as with any question you should respond with honesty. If you do work well under pressure, describe specific situations where you have handled pressure well and what you did to do so. Once again be sure to not discuss any negative details of those examples which would tear down the reputation of others or another company.

If it is true, discuss how level headed you are when facing pressure and stress. You can talk about practices you partake in to lower your stress level and deliver your requirements in a timely manner. If at all possible you can talk about how your cool and calm demeanor helps a team and how it helps others in the workplace around you.

If you do not work well under pressure do not pretend that you do. This will not automatically take you out of the running for employment so long as you respond in a way which is positive. Rather than saying you are terrible under pressure, and begin describing ways in which pressure has made you fail in your position, respond in a way which explains what you need in order to work.

Providing details on what helps you be successful in high pressure situations will allow the employer to see you do not simply wander aimlessly. If you are able to be proactive and begin the process of defusing any stress, the employer will view this in a positive manner. Rather than stating you work terribly under stress and timelines focus on speaking about times in which you were able to still succeed with the leadership of your team leader or supervisor and the specific actions which were taken.

It would also be advisable to communicate with your perspective employer that you do not work well under pressure and because of that you have learned you are one who needs clear communication and work best when planning far in advance. There is not an employer in the world who would say good communication and advanced planning are bad for a team dynamic or working under stress.

When responding to this question avoid talking about situations or details as to why you have disliked your last positions. This will only allow the potential employer an opportunity to compare and contrast how your last positions are similar to the one for which you are applying. If the employer is able to find enough similarities which you have a personal distaste then it is highly likely you will be taking out of consideration for the position in question.

Regardless of your response in any question avoid using curse words or derogatory comments. Even if you feel they are warranted they are always unprofessional and will only paint you in a bad light rather than helping to describe the situation in your favor. In the same manner avoid speaking poorly of anyone you have worked with in the past or the companies for which you have been employed.

In the same vain ensure you do not talk negatively about those you have worked with and how they had a poor impact on your work ethic or created more stress or pressure. Instead speak on how those situations were effectively diffused. Do not speak about times in which deadlines were not met or you gave in poorly to pressure unless you are asked specifically.

Describe A Situation Where You Were The Focal Point

Employers who ask this question are wanting to find out how quick you are to think on your feet and if you are a good problem solver. They are also searching for an ability to avoid creating stressful situations and an ability to make proper choices which benefit the company in the long run. The employer will often use this question as a way to dig deeper into your ability to deal with high pressure situations.

Spend your time talking about times in which you were able to think quickly and work fast to solve a problem on your own which helped the company or prevented issues from arising. If you are able to give a few examples you can provide them at that time. Companies are always looking for people who have an ability to work seamlessly between being a team player and working well on their own.

It would be advised to speak about your problem-solving abilities and give examples where you made correct choices where the supervisor did not need to be involved. Elaborate on your talents and how those talents have helped in situations where you needed to act quickly in a high-pressure situation. If you are unable to do this speak on situations where you were able to work with a team to solve the issue and what steps were taken.

You can also speak about having been proactive when a

situation was rising and your effective communication with your team and supervisor. Describe once again how you feel effective communication, planning ahead and being prepared are important for your personal success and the success of the company.

Do your best to refrain from talking about situations where you were the cause of the issue or made the situation more difficult. If you place yourself at the center of the problem this may cause the potential employer to be concerned that you will behave in this manner again and cause more issues down the road. An employer will see patterns of past behavior which go against their desired work ethic as a negative.

Instead speak on situations where you were positive about a difficult situation and either helped lead others to a solution or were able to take direction. If you can state any examples where you were left to make choices for yourself without the guidance of others this will help demonstrate your ability to work well on your own. Employers are excited about employees who can think for themselves but are not afraid to approach leadership in situations in which they may be unable to come to a conclusion on their own.

Describe A Situation Where You Had To Deal With Your Manager

Employers asking this type of question are doing so in the hopes of understanding the dynamic in your relationships with supervisors in past positions. Your best practice in this case is to speak clearly about your relationship with your supervisor in a positive and uplifting manner. Focusing on the positive aspects of working with leadership will demonstrate your ability to work with a manager.

When discussing the details of your relationship and the situation, focus on the positive aspects of working with your previous boss. In what ways had your boss helped you in the past? Where there times in which your employer was helpful to you and aided your learning in your position of employment?

If there are times in which you gained valuable mentor ship with your boss, responding with that information to this question would be a wonderful way to show the positive side of your work under supervision. Being able to speak about what things you enjoyed about working with your last boss will help your potential employer understand that you find value in working symbiotically with your supervisor.

Were there times in which your supervisor was able to provide to you valuable education or tools which you had not previously experienced? If so you should elaborate on those and how grateful you were for their guidance. Employers are searching for employees who find value in the people with whom the employees are working closely.

Avoid speaking poorly of the relationship with your previous boss or the company. As always this only will show your potential employer a negative outlook for the position and company which you previously had. Instead focus on the aspects of the position you enjoyed.

If you are able to use a specific example of a time in which you needed to work closely with your manager or the manager was needed to diffuse a situation which could not be handled on your own, focus on the details of the story which show your ability to problem solve and follow instructions. If at all possible describe how that particular situation was pivotal in your growth and learning process. It will be even more impactful in your interview if you are able to describe how your positive relationship with your boss made the situation even more valuable.

If the relationship you had with your previous boss was

not positive it would be wise to try and find aspects which were positive or take the negative and word things in a positive manner. Using words like, team work, positive impact, and learning experience will help keep the conversation positive without appearing as though you are trying to disguise the negative experiences.

When describing your examples do not make up stories or attempt to fill the story with untruthful additives in order to coordinate your response to the question at hand. Do your best to remain as truthful about the situation as you can. Should you fall into the trap of fictionalizing your experience and your potential employer is able to find out this information through conversations with your previous employer this will reflect poorly on your character. If the stories you have to share do not seem to be detailed enough remember it is better to be truthful than to be caught in a lie.

CHAPTER 9

THE WORST THINGS YOU CAN DO

By now, you should feel confident and well-prepared for any upcoming job interview. In addition to all the crucial elements that have been covered, here are 12 more often overlooked factors, some of which are minor issues and others absolute no-no's, that could easily ruin your chances of landing your dream job. After all, an interview is the last chance you will get to convince an employer why you are the best fit for their company, so make this crucial opportunity count.

01. Showing up late.

If you arrive for an interview later than the appointed time, you are already off to a bad start. Being punctual should be at the top of the list when it comes to making a good first impression.

02. Get caught lying.

A definite guarantee that you will not get the job is to lie during the job interview. If you are going to make a bold claim or state something that is not true, seriously think about your chances of getting away with it. Companies run background checks on potential hires. Whether it is about your credentials, accomplishments or your work history, honesty will usually be the best policy.

03. Forgetting common courtesy.

Did you greet the interviewer politely with a smile and a firm handshake? When the interview ended did you give another handshake and thank the interviewer for their time? If you did not do any of those, do not be surprised if you do not hear back from the potential employer again. Interviewers gather clues about candidates based on whether they are punctual, how they are dressed, the eye contact they make and the words they use. A minor slip up, such not maintaining basic manners, can cost you dearly.

04. Straying too far from a question.

As questions are being asked, keep your answers to the point and relevant to the context of the interview. It also helps to provide specific examples to support your answers, such as talking about a scenario that happened in the past to illustrate your skills and accomplishments.

The important thing to remember is to keep things directly related to the questions being asked and not go off topic.

05. Inappropriate humor.

Be confident, but avoid cracking jokes unnecessarily or saying things probably best left unsaid. A little touch of humor could work in your favor, provided that it is appropriate to the context of the interview. You do not need to be funny, especially when it is at the expense of appropriateness and formality. The last thing you want is for the hiring manager to think you are not serious about the job opportunity.

06. Getting personal.

A job interview is a formal meeting to assess if you are the right fit for a job. Everything in your personal life, your subjective opinions and how you are feeling should be left outside the door, and not be brought up during the interview.

07. Appearing arrogant and entitled.

No one owes you a job; you have to earn the opportunity. If you really are the right candidate for the job, your credentials and professionalism will speak for itself. You appear full of yourself if you make inflated claims about your qualifications, bad mouth previous employers or make assumptions about the job role.

08. Not appearing attentive.

It goes without saying that you should give 101% of your attention to the interviewer and respond to questions accordingly. Not smiling, playing with something on the table, bad posture, no eye contact, and fidgeting too much are behaviors indicating you are not paying attention. Additionally, checking your phone or answering calls are almost definitely job interview deal breakers.

09. Mind your language.

Keep your language formal and professional. Avoid cursing, profanity and "cute" remarks ("My wife wants me to get this job"); you may think you are being witty and funny, but the interviewer will take it as rude and a lack of professionalism. The same thing should apply to your tone of speech. That means no speaking loudly or remarks which could be perceived as impolite.

10. Saying more than you have to.

Shakespeare once said that "Brevity is the soul of wit", and he is absolutely right. So, answer whatever is asked of you by the interviewer and avoid rambling on.

11. Bringing an entourage.

You are the one who will be interviewed; there is no need for any pomp and pageantry. Family members, friends and significant others – no matter how well-meaning they might be – should not accompany you when you are going for a job interview. There have even been extreme cases of people bringing their pets along - do not do that.

12. Ask when the interview will end.

Nothing says "I don't care about this job and I am just wasting your time" like asking the interviewer how long the interview will be, or when will it end. You will also be doing just as much damage by constantly looking at your watch. When you are called in for a job interview, you are expected to make time for it, if you really want to get the job.

CHAPTER 10

HOW DO I ANSWER DIFFICULT AND AWKWARD QUESTIONS?

In this Chapter we'll explore why you may be asked difficult or awkward questions, give some examples and the best responses.

The best way of dealing with difficult questions is to be well prepared, relaxed and confident, so be sure to cash in on your preparation work by using it.

Why you may be asked difficult questions

Let's think about it, why would your interviewer deliberately ask you difficult or awkward questions?

> To make you look stupid.

> To make you feel uncomfortable.

> To trick you into looking foolish.

> To put you down in some way.

> To stress you out.

> To reduce you to a gibbering wreck.

I don't think so, do you? And, if he or she keeps on doing it, they may not be in their job too long).

On the other hand, if it becomes clear to you that the interviewer is deliberately using stress interviewing techniques on you (e.g. being aggressive, shouting, not letting you answer a question before asking another, being offensive), you may need to make a decision:

.....unless handling that sort of interaction is part of the job, do you really want to work for a company like that?

The value system your answer displays would be highly valued by most companies and you will likely have impressed the interviewer.

If you have answered in a relaxed manner, you will likely have maintained rapport and demonstrated your unflappability.

Great job, well done.

If the interviewer presses harder with follow-up questions designed to cause you to break confidence, recognize that your morals and character may be being tested.

Stay calm (e.g. use your breathing) and stay consistent in choosing your integrity as your top priority.

You will win the respect of the interviewer.

Here are some examples of difficult and awkward questions that you may encounter:

* which is more important to you, money or job satisfaction?

as illustrated above, you may have to reframe or qualify questions that pose an unfair choice like this by saying something along the lines of:

"whilst both are important to me, one may assume priority over the other depending on the circumstances.

For example, if I was a young married man with small children, the money may be critical in providing a decent lifestyle for my family.

But, assuming I have enough money for my needs, job satisfaction is much more important to me".

* the non-verbal question - a pause - which the interviewer extends out into a lengthy intimidating silence

Stay calm, as if thinking and then (smile? and) say, "do you need any further details or examples in answer to your last question?"

* tell me about the most boring job you've ever had

this is an opportunity to show the interviewer that you are proactive in a job and don't accept low standards.

For example, you might say:

"well every job has its more exciting and less exciting bits, I suppose, but I never get bored at work. I enjoy being busy and hard work and I always find something to do.

I think if people are bored they probably aren't using their brain enough, for example in learning more about the job or coming up with ideas to improve things or communicating with others in the team".

* would you rather be liked or feared?

Again, the pattern of not literally answering the question as posed works well with this sort of question.

For example, "on reflection, I think neither, I'd rather be respected by others because that's a better way to exert influence, build relationships and achieve great results".

* on a scale of 1-10 how would you rate me as an

interviewer?

Stay positive, pick out an element of the interview that you can give positive feedback about, and do - sincerely.

For example:

"I have enjoyed our interview and you have made it easy for me to talk. I think you have been very thorough and professional". Ignore the request for a numerical rating.

* have you done your best work in your current role?

Your answer must be, "yes", but you can't stop there as the implication is that for the future maybe your new employer isn't going to get your best (where do you go from "best"?).

So, you would have to go on to say that just like a sportsperson keeps doing and improving their best, you have a similar attitude and you would expect to be better tomorrow than you are today (through continuously learning, problem solving, great teamwork etc. - re-iterate those key elements that the job demands which you identified in your preparation).

* What will you do if you don't get this position?

use this question as an opportunity to show that you are well organized, resilient, willing to learn and resourceful.

For example, you might say something like:

"I would be very disappointed, of course, as I believe I am a great match for the job and I am keen to work with a progressive employer such as you, but I would obviously respect your decision.

I would ask for some feedback from you, if possible, to help me learn from this experience.

Then I would review my goals and plan, make any necessary changes and pursue my campaign to get my ideal job with renewed vigor.

I know I will make a valuable contribution based on my career and experiences to date".

Go back to your preparation and make a list of the questions (from your C.V. / resume) you would regard as difficult.

Examine the above and re-iterate the pattern that answering difficult questions is a great opportunity which nearly always requires you to impress the interviewer by reframing the question.

In particular, what you answer will impress if the

interviewer can see that you are using your brain and being genuine (he or she knows you are not perfect, you're a person).

How you answer will impress the interviewer if he or she can see that you avoid getting ruffled, stay relaxed and don't compromise your key values (especially, integrity).

In Summary:

* the interviewer has a purpose in asking you difficult or awkward questions and it is not to "destroy" you (unless handling that is part of the job you've applied for).

If his or her reason is to be destructive, you may decide that you don't want to work in that company

* the interviewer is usually looking for two levels of response - 1. what you say interns of the question asked and 2. how you answer in terms of your values and integrity

* don't compromise your integrity, the interviewer may be testing whether you will "cave in" under pressure or whether you will stick to your guns on significant points.

Exercises to Do:

* from your preparation materials, compile a list of difficult or awkward questions that you may be asked.

Create possible answers that will address the interviewer's two-tier purpose and impress

* practice answering these difficult questions (with a range of different potential impressive answers) out loud (alone or with a friend), record your efforts and review them for learnings in terms of start doing, stop doing and do differently.

CHAPTER 11

THE BASIC DOCUMENTS

The application part of the process is really just a simple exchange of information between the recruiter and the candidate. The recruiter will provide you with one or more documents outlining the job and what they are seeking in a candidate, and in return you will provide them with a reply showing how you fulfil the requirements they are looking for. I realize that this seems simple to the point of being patronizing, but it is amazing how many people seem to overlook the relationship between the information that the recruit provides and what information the candidate needs to give in return.

As I said, the recruiter will provide you with one or more documents, these days usually via their website. The information that the recruiter provides can be broken down into four areas or documents: the advert, the job description, the personal specification and the application form. Some organizations will be very kind and provide you with all four as separate documents, while others will bundle the first three into a single document. All of these documents will provide you with insight into what they are looking for in the perfect candidate. Let's have a look at each in a bit more detail.

The Advert

The advert is the short snappy text that is designed to catch your eye and draw you in to read more. Depending on the size and type of organization doing the recruiting, the advert may tell you little about the specific job and more about the company, for example "A global leader in the button making industry, we employ over 45,000 people in 104 different countries". The advert should act as the executive summary for everything that follows, highlighting who the organization is, what the specific job role is, the key qualifications, skills and experiences they are looking for, and the details of the post (e.g. salary, location, hours and contract type).

It is important to take note of any qualifications, skills and experience that appear in the advert. The recruiter usually has a limited amount of text to play with so any requirements that appear are likely to be right at the top of their wish list. For instance, if the advert starts with "Are you a university graduate with a passion for boat building..." you can be pretty confident that they are after someone with a university degree.

The Job Description

A good job description should allow you to build a picture in your mind of what your life would be like if you were successful in getting this job. You should be able to start with the high-level information (similar to the details in the advert if it was given as a separate document) such as where you will be working, who you will be working for (usually termed line manager or "reporting to"), if the job involves management of others (usually termed line management or direct reports) and the area of work. You can then go deeper and get an idea of what your responsibilities will be. Most organizations label these as duties or responsibilities and tend to lay them out in bullet point format.

The Personal Specification

In my mind, the personal specification is the most important of all the information you will be given about a prospective job. It tells you exactly what the employer is looking for in an applicant and can very quickly tell you if it is worth you expending time and energy applying for the post. When I am looking at jobs, once the advert has got me interested, I tend to jump straight to the personal specification to get a sense of the type of person they are after.

Most public sector organizations (councils, higher education, NHS, etc.) provide a separate document or a section at the end of the job description detailing the personal specification, which is incredibly helpful. Others bundle it in with the text job description which means you have to work a bit harder to find the information. If they are feeling really helpful, they will split the list of requirements into those that are essential and those which are desirable (more about this shortly).

The personal specification is essentially a list of what the perfect candidate looks like. This is often split into groups under specific headings. Different companies use different groupings but for the purpose of this book, I will stick with the three most common, namely qualifications, experience and skills.

Qualifications. Common alternative terms used to describe qualifications in a personal specification are education, accomplishments and training. Qualifications can be viewed as things you have a piece of paper to prove you've done (e.g. GCSEs, A Levels, NVQs, university degrees, diplomas). They are binary: either you have them or you don't.

Experience. Experience is sometimes categorized as knowledge or competencies, and some organizations actually separate experience and knowledge into separate groups, which always seemed odd to me as most people gain their knowledge from a combination of their education and experiences.

Experience simply relates to things you have done. Some experience is directly tied to the skills that the recruiter is looking for. For example, if a company is looking for someone with presentation skills, it is likely they will want that individual to have had the experience of doing formal presentations. Others will be more generic, such as experience of the healthcare system or experience dealing with foreign companies.

Skills. Skills are often categorized as attributes, abilities or qualities in personal specifications or job adverts. If experience is what you have done, then skills are things you can do, or your ability to do a specific task well. They are far more fluid than qualifications and so it is much harder to prove or disprove that someone has a given skill. As a result, skills are often judged based on examples of your work as evidence that you possess that skill. Sometimes skills can be turned into a qualification which acts as hard evidence that you not only have the skill but you have reached a level of proficiency that means someone is willing to certify you as competent. A good example of this is project management. Most of us have had experience of managing projects in our day-to-day lives, whether it is having an extension built at home or implementing a new IT system at work, and so many people will claim it among their skills, but those who have put the time and effort into getting a certified project management qualification (e.g. PRINCE2) will always have the edge.

Sticking with the example of project management, here is a version of a personal specification for a recently advertised project management post. I've removed a lot of the content as it was three pages long, but it should give a good illustration of what a personal specification can look like. Note that before the specification itself there is an "evidence how" key. This tells you if the recruiting manager expects you to show that you meet the criteria in your application (A), at interview (I) or as part of a test (T), likely done at interview. This is worth paying close attention to. If there are criteria that are specifically labelled as "A" for application, you will need to make sure that you cover these as part of your application.

Application Forms

Not all organizations will provide an application form to be completed. For some, submitting a copy of your CV and a covering letter will be enough. However, where there is an application form, take the time to look over it as it may provide you with some clues as to what the recruiters are after. Beyond all of the generic information you need to fill out (e.g. your details, education history, job history) look to see if there are any free text short answer questions they want you to complete and if so, what the subject area of the question is. If they ask you to answer a question about the importance of customer service, make a mental note that you'll need to emphasize your customer service skills and experience (and qualifications should you have them) throughout your application.

Now we've covered the basics, let's work through the process of identifying and applying for a job.

Let's review the key points we have covered in this chapter.

The organization that is recruiting will provide a number of documents to prospective candidates, which usually take the form of a job advert, a job description, a personal specification and an application form.

Some organizations will provide all of these documents, while others may only provide one or two, and may combine them into one document.

Job adverts often provide clues as to the recruiter's top priorities, so you should take note of these and see how they compare to your qualifications, skills and experience.

- A well-written job description should allow you to start to build a picture in your mind as to what the job would be like on a day-to-day basis. It will outline the key tasks the employee would be expected to do and what the main responsibilities of the role would be (e.g. line management responsibilities).

- The personal specification is the most useful of all the documents in helping you decide if this is a job worthy of your attention. It should tell you exactly what the employer is looking for from a candidate and thus the criteria that you will be judged against during shortlisting.

- Most personal specifications separate the attributes they are looking for into qualifications, skills and experience. It should only take a few minutes to look at a personal specification and get a sense of whether it is worth you giving it further consideration.

- Sometimes companies will provide a pre-formatted application form. If there is one, have a quick look to see what sort of questions they ask. This can give you a hint as to their priorities.

CHAPTER 12

JOB INTERVIEW QUESTIONS ON WORKING WITH PEOPLE

Are you a team player?

The answer to this question must be in the affirmative because there is hardly a position that does not require team spirit, though the levels of the requirement do vary. As a matter of fact, this question should be answered with enthusiasm in order to show that you are truly passionate about working with others as a team. However, your answer should be justified with an example.

Sample Answer

I read in a book that the word, 'TEAM' is the acronym for Together Each Achieves More. Being a team player is a requisite for enhanced productivity. One of the best benefits of working in a team is that it affords people the opportunity of learning from one another because no one knows it all. I have the experience of working as a member of a team in some organizations, in my church and in my community development union and I enjoyed them.

Do you prefer working independently or on a team?

This question may be a follow-up to the one above. While asking this question, the interviewer is interested in finding out if you are really a team player. Being a good team player, however, does not imply that you will not be able to perform excellently in tasks that do not require team work. You should emphasize your ability to perform well in both, especially if you do not know if you will work alone or with people if you are employed. Besides, working alone and working with people are often required for any position in an organization.

Sample Answer

I do well as a member of a team in projects that require working with people. I also do well in tasks I am expected to work independently. I enjoy both.

Can you give an example of a team you worked with?

Sample Answer

I was a member of the team that reviewed the activities of the marketing department of the last organization I worked with.

How do you feel working in a team?

This question may be inevitable if the job you applied for requires team work. You should answer this question with enthusiasm and passion.

Sample Answers

I enjoy working in a team and I easily get along with others.

A work environment that requires team work is usually the ideal for every worker because it affords people the opportunity to learn from one another. This is why I am always very happy working in a team.

What are your experiences with working with a team?

Sample Answers

With the aid of my experience as a member of different teams at different places and different times, I have realized that one of the most difficult aspects of work in any organization is relating with people, especially when they lack common interest.

From experience, I observed that different people have different ideologies and perceptions of reality. Sometimes, these differences are irreconcilable. Worse still, some people in a team always want things to be done in a way they like, even if their teammates dislike it.

What do your colleagues usually complain about you when you work with them in a team?

While asking this question, the interviewer wants to know how sensitive you are to people's feelings about you. He also wants to know if people's criticisms make sense to you. Best answers to this question are usually the type that shows that your colleagues are unable to meet your high standards.

Sample Answers

I enjoy getting people's comments about me because they help me to know the areas of life I am doing well, and the areas I need to improve on. My colleagues always complain that I have abnormal standards which are unusual and difficult for others to accept as they are too high for them.

My colleagues often complain that I always have a radical departure from conventional thinking, which, though, often makes sense.

What are your expectations from your colleagues when you are working together on a project?

Sample Answers

I expect them to subordinate their personal interests to that of the team. I expect them to see the success of the team as the superior goal.

Whenever I work with people in a team, I expect them to cooperate with others so that they will not frustrate the efforts of their teammates.

What type of colleagues do you love working with?

Sample Answer

I easily get along with people and I always do my job with seriousness. I love colleagues who are easy to get along with and who also treat their job with seriousness. Such colleagues eliminate unnecessary stress in a place of work. As a matter of fact, they help to make a job a hobby rather than a burden.

How would your colleagues describe you?

The interviewer asks this question in order to ascertain your perception of your colleagues' thoughts about you.

Sample Answers

My colleagues see me as a catalyst in a team who easily inspires others to get things done faster and better.

My colleagues see me as a goal getter.

My colleagues see me as someone who has high value for time.

What do you dislike most about your colleagues / teammates?

Emphasize an attitude that would affect a team negatively and which others would also hate about you in a team.

Sample Answers

What I dislike most about my colleagues is deliberately frustrating the efforts of others when we ought to be working towards a common goal.

I dislike my colleagues being selfish and insensitive to the feelings of others.

What do you do when you work with a colleague who is difficult to get along with?

This question is geared towards finding out how tolerant and mature you are in relating with your colleagues, especially when they are difficult to get along with. Avoid giving the impression that you react to them in a harsh way. Also avoid giving the impression that you exhibit absolute tolerance to them because you will never be able to help them with such attitude.

Sample Answers

I have learnt from experience that it is wrong to judge what people do without understanding why they do so. Sometimes, someone's bad experience in his private life could incapacitate him from relating effectively with people at his place of work. Hence, when it is difficult to get along with a colleague, I try to unveil the factors that are responsible for that. When I achieve that, I try as much as I can to assist him overcome the challenge.

I have worked with a problem colleague but I applied high level of maturity in managing the relationship. I try to tolerate such person as much as I can, bearing in mind that there are some weaknesses I have he may also be tolerating, which I may be ignorant of. However,

I try to call him to order in a prudent way when his attitudes constitute a threat to achieving organizational goals.

How do you get along with older/younger colleagues?

This question will be tailored to your situation. You may be asked how you get along with older colleagues if most of the people you will work with in the organization, if you are offered appointment, are older than you are. If, however, you will work with younger people, the question would be reversed.

Sample Answers

Working with people in an organization is always a challenge, irrespective of whether they are older or younger than you are. One of the major challenges of working with older workers is that they are hardly tolerant of change. Hence, I always I apply caution when recommending new ways of doing things. I make such recommendation through the appropriate channel at the appropriate time, but also respect their feelings when my ideas are unacceptable to them.

Working with younger people often requires patience

and tolerance, especially when they are fresh graduates. I try as much as I can to accommodate them in a way that does not jeopardize organizational goals.

Have you ever been of help to a colleague in any of the organizations you with?

Sample Answers

Angela was a colleague of mine who was always committed to her duties in the organization. All of a sudden, her attitudes to work became very poor. That made it very difficult to work with her. She almost frustrated her colleagues who worked with her in a team on a project that had a deadline. Our colleagues complained about that but I encouraged them not to allow her attitudes to make us not to achieve our goal. They listened to me. When I spoke to her at the end of the project, I realized that her marriage had just broken, and that was responsible for her ugly attitudes towards her job. I blamed her for not confiding in anyone. However, I counseled her until she started picking up gradually.

Philip was a colleague of mine who had lackadaisical attitude to his job. He did what he ought to do only when he was being supervised. I observed that doing so was part of him. I took time to make him understand that what he was doing profits neither himself nor the organization. I also made him understand that he was doing worse harm to himself by not being serious with his job. I was happy that his attitude to work changed for the better when he realized the dangers of his negative attitude to work.

Have you worked with someone you did not like, or someone who did not like you?

The reason the interviewer asks this question is that he is interested in finding out if you allow your personal relationship with your colleagues to affect your obligations to your employer.

Sample Answer

I once had a colleague who did not like me. Though cordial relationship between colleagues is always encouraged as it helps workers to build a home in their places of work, the performance of the duties of employees is more important than their relationship with themselves. When every trick I employed to create an effective relationship with him failed, I focused single mindedly on my tasks in the organization. His hatred would have been worrisome if it had affected my work in the organization. I was consoled when I discovered that he also had difficulty getting along with most of our colleagues in the organization.

What would your past colleagues say is your greatest weakness?

While answering this question, do not cite a negative quality you have. Rather, present one of your strengths as a weakness. You may also cite a weakness you have that has nothing to do with the position you applied for.

Sample Answer

My colleagues know me as someone who expects much from the people he works with at all times.

What would your past colleagues say is your greatest strength?

It would be in your own interest to emphasize qualities that are relevant to the position you applied for.

Sample Answers

They know me as a trustworthy person who can be confided in without any fear of betrayal. (This answer is very suitable for someone who is applying for a position that requires confidentiality e.g. confidential secretary).

My past colleagues know me as someone who is organized and who has exceptional leadership skills. (This answer is very suitable for someone who is applying for a position that requires administration and leadership).

Have you ever had misunderstanding with a colleague?

Do not pretend to be a perfect person who has perfect relationship with every colleague. It is imperative to remark that it is difficult, if not impossible, not to have had misunderstanding with at least one colleague if you have put in some years in service. Having misunderstanding with a colleague does not necessarily imply that you are a bad employee, as you may not be the cause of the problem. The goal of the interviewer while asking this question is to test your maturity and ability to manage conflicts, especially in your place of work. The interviewer expects you to be sensitive of people's weaknesses. He also expects you to influence your colleagues positively. Do not complain about people or remark that you try to avoid them. You should be as diplomatic as you can while answering this question.

Sample Answer

Misunderstanding is inevitable anywhere people interact. It is difficult not to have had a misunderstanding with one's colleagues in a place of work, especially when one has worked for some years. Misunderstanding provides an opportunity for people to exhibit how mature they are. I try to manage the situation with maturity whenever it occurs.

In your opinion, could there be any benefit from having a misunderstanding with your colleague?

Sample Answer

In addition to providing an opportunity for people to exhibit how mature they are, misunderstanding in a place of work also provides an opportunity for people to understand their colleagues better.

What do your colleagues love most about you?

Sample Answer

They appreciate my ability to instill passion in others.

What do you love most about your colleagues?

Sample Answer

What I appreciate most in my colleagues is cooperating

with others to achieve a common goal. I am very delighted with colleagues who subordinate their personal goals to common goals.

How did you feel giving information that led to the dismissal of your colleague?

Tell the interviewer if you have not had such experience before. However, if you have ever done such, you should give a reasonable explanation for the action. The interviewer wants to know if your loyalty to your employer is superior to your loyalty to your colleagues.

Sample Answer

I felt bad about that, but I had no alternative option. He was defrauding the company. I advised him several times that what he was doing could put him in trouble, in addition to risking the collapse of the company. I was forced to report him as I did not want to be part of the evil.

Have you ever been a problem employee?

The answer to this question must not be in the affirmative for any reason if you want to get the job.

Sample Answer

I have never been a problem employee and I will never be that type of an employee in any organization at any time.

Have you ever disciplined a problem subordinate?

This question may be inevitable if the position you applied for requires supervisory roles. It may also be inevitable if the organization has zero-tolerance to indiscipline. The interviewer may also ask this question if he is convinced that you are too kind-hearted to discipline a problem subordinate. It is imperative to remark that organizational goals will likely be betrayed (always) if sanctions are not adequately enforced. Hence, you should be willing to discipline your subordinates whenever the need for that arises, just as your superiors would be willing to discipline you when you violate the laws of the organization.

Sample Answer

I was compelled to discipline a problem employee when every effort to call him to order proved abortive.

In what ways will you discipline a problem subordinate?

Do not say that you will bring in new disciplinary measures with your personal initiative. Rather, promise to adhere very strictly to the policy of the organization on disciplining staff who violate the rules and regulations of the company.

Sample Answer

Disciplinary actions usually depend on the offence committed. I believe the organization has prescribed penalties for different categories of offences. These prescriptions will determine the disciplinary measure I will take on a problem staff. However, I believe that cautioning the staff should be a step before discipline.

What do you do after disciplining a subordinate?

Sample Answer

I try to let him understand in a prudent way that the disciplinary action was in his interest and that of the organization and his colleagues.

How do you feel working with a staff after disciplining him?

Sample Answer

My primary concern is doing what is right, not with how

the person feels about it or how he feels towards me.

What do people say about you?

You should be very mindful of the fact that though every human being is a different person to different people, there are some things people know about you. You should also be mindful of the fact that what you claim that people say about you is expected to reflect in your life style if you are offered appointment by the organization.

Sample Answers

Most of my associates easily describe me as a goal-oriented person.

Many people describe me as a goal-getter.

A lot of people say that I am a very principled person.

Are there people who hate you?

Sample Answer

I sincerely believe that it is not possible to be loved by everyone. So, there are people who hate me, just as there are also those who love me. But I think there are more people who love me than those who hate me.

This answer may lead to another question, "Why do you think that it is not possible to be loved by all?"

Sample Answer

Every human being is a different person to different persons. I believe the important thing in life is not that you are loved by someone, but the reason you are loved by the person. I do not see someone as an evil person because another person hates him. The reason is that I am more interested in why the person is not loved. It is difficult to be loved by evil people if you do not support them. It is also difficult to be hated by good people if you are good.

CHAPTER 13

QUESTIONS WITH A HIDDEN MEANING AT THE INTERVIEW

Often, in response to the employer's questions, candidates say something that should present them in a good light. To learn about the job seeker more than he wants to say, recruiters can ask specific cunning questions.

Many of the applicants before the interview study possible questions and prepare answers to them. However, an employer can not simply ask the question directly, but make it so that the candidate does not understand his true intentions. The recruiter can also start a conversation with general topics to get your good feeling, and then use the tricky questions to find out accurate information.

HRs know that in the analysis of the candidate it is important to know the level of his self-esteem. It can serve as a starting point for predicting his future behavior on the job. But everyone believes that he estimates himself correctly. At this, special questions can give a recruiter more precise information:

- "Tell us about your successes". Candidates are more open to respond to the word "success" rather than "achievement" considering that the achievements can only be in leadership positions. Therefore, namely such a question can get you to open up. If you cannot answer this question, the employer decides that you are either too modest or cannot carry out your work at the proper level.

- "Have you ever been denied employment? If - yes, what do you think, why?". This is a very awkward question, but it allows the employer to accurately determine your self-esteem by comparing your thoughts on this issue and details of the experience and skills.

- "In what team do you feel most comfortable?" If you say that you prefer to work in a team of professionals, most likely, you are not afraid of competition, you have leadership skills and high self-esteem. Note that high self-esteem should go together with good skills and achievements. If you say that you prefer the friendly staff, then the teamwork is not option for you. It can also mean that for the work you need support and help of colleagues.

- The reasons why a candidate changed his places of work, define much - his values, degree of proneness to conflict, etc. Direct question can be followed by a socially acceptable answer - lack of career development, for example. Therefore, the recruiter can go the other way:

- "How do you feel about the changes? What motivates you to change something in your life?" It turns out that not your weaknesses are discussed but your general principles of life. And on this subject, you can philosophize more sincerely. In this case, expect the also clarifying questions.

- "How do you think why employees change jobs?" Again, this question will withdraw you from the idea that the question is directed namely to your personality and your potential weaknesses. You answer as if about others, but starting from your own experience.

- "On what parameters did you choose the previous places of work?". Then clarifying questions will follow: "What has changed since the beginning of your work?", "What were the pros and cons?", etc. Again, focus here is not specifically on your personality, so HR can expect more truthful answers that easily characterize you.

Remember that first and foremost the employer assesses you, as if he did not. This is not the whole list of possible questions with a hidden meaning, but it will give you a general idea about the intentions and methods, which may be used by the interviewer.

As it is known, there are result-oriented and the process-oriented employees. Result orientation implies that the fruits of work can be measured both quantitatively and qualitatively. Results-orientation first of all is needed for middle managers and senior managers, PR- and HR-managers, marketers, salespeople, real estate agents and other employees whose salary depends on completed transactions. Staff focused on the process is more than inclined to perform repetitive operations. They are more motivated to stability, prefer a definite schedule.

It is believed to be result-oriented is more prestigious, although this is not always true. Therefore, to the recruiter' direct question: "What is more important to you: the work process or the result of work" the applicant will reply that the result is more important, although this may not be the case. But employers have other options:

- "Tell me how you were looking for previous work" A candidate who is more focused on the results of work, will describe the process of job search with a few highlights, and will not go into details. Candidate oriented mostly on the process will describe everything in detail: CV writing, publishing it, responses to the vacancies, passing through interviews, etc.

- "What should be your ideal vacation?" Employee focusing on results will tell where he will go, what impressions he expects, what sights he wants to see, i.e. will accurately describe the final result. A person aimed at the process will pay more attention to the description of how he wants to spend time swimming, sunbathing, spend time with the kids, etc.

- "Do you do sports?" According to the observations, the people who are actively involved in sports are more focused on results. Also, it is considered if it is a team sport or an individual.

How a candidate builds relationships to colleagues and superiors? Whether he is inclined to conflicts? It is not difficult to imagine how a competitor will answer such direct questions. But experienced recruiters know how to ask rightly:

- "Describe your former leaders". The recruiter will not ask to call the names and companies but will ask to give only general characteristics. From the responses of the candidate it will be possible to understand what type of leaders is more convenient for him to work with, what qualities the candidate values, and which not. This will help to understand whether a future employee will pull together with leadership in the new workplace.

- "What would you do to find a common language with the leadership?" This is a difficult question that will make you think. And because of the limitations of time, you most likely will answer based on past experience. The answers will help the employer to determine your personal qualities: communication skills, proneness to conflict, loyalty, etc.

- "Was the staff considered valuable on your previous jobs and how it was manifested or was not manifested?" In this question, attention is transferred from the candidate to the former companies and colleagues, which increases the likelihood of more honest answers. The candidate will answer based on personal opinion, his own principles, impressions and experiences, and this will provide valuable information.

Remember that employer may well talk with you about abstract topics, but the answers will tell a lot about you as a person. No matter how the questions are built, the employer is interested in revealing your qualities, rather than how bad was your former manager.

CHAPTER 14

EVALUATING THE ORGANIZATION

In the middle of their mock interview, Charles asked Jessica for the most challenging or frustrating thing about her current job. Jessica, who is a very friendly and bubbly person, remarked that there wasn't anything frustrating about her job because she worked at a spa and her customers were always happy. She wrapped up her answer by comparing this situation to her last job, at a big box office supply retailer. Intrigued by the comparison, Charles asked about that previous experience. Jessica told him, "The customers get really upset sometimes, like really angry." According to Jessica, many customers had problems with the products, certain company policies were unethical, and its employees weren't treated well. After describing these experiences, she said, "It was a great comparison. Now I know what a real job that cares is like, and I know what a job that doesn't care is like." In the future, Jessica might evaluate the reputation of the organization and learn about its policies before accepting a job.

One of your two responsibilities during the interview is to figure out whether you really do want the job. Regardless of how much you already know about the organization, the people who work there, and the job itself, you can always learn more. Unfortunately, you'll never know with absolute certainty if the job and the organization are a perfect fit for you before you start working there. But taking the time to evaluate whether you might be satisfied and happy in an organization and in a specific job will weed out a lot of bad experiences like the one that Jessica described above.

Research Starts Early

Ideally, researching an organization should begin before you apply for a job. But whenever you start the process—before deciding to apply, while targeting your resume to the job, before your interview, or after it— there are many good ways to learn about an organization.

Read the Job Ad

There is often a section at the beginning or end of the job ad that describes the company and its employees. It may say things like "Fast-paced start-up is looking for…"; this communicates that they're looking for an employee who will work hard and be comfortable with change. Or it could say, "We're a Fortune 500 company..." in order to let you know that they are a very big company with a lot of revenue.

Read the Organization's Website

You don't have to read its entire website, but certain pages may be very useful in finding details about an organization, especially one you're not very familiar with. The website should be useful for answering questions like:

- How is the organization structured? Is it for-profit or nonprofit, publically traded or private, run by a single person, a small partnership, a family, or a cooperative?

- How does the organization earn money? Who gives money to whom? Which functional units make money, and which seem like they might cost more money than they bring in?

- Who are the senior managers or leaders? Who are the managers and coworkers you might have daily interactions with? What are the backgrounds of these people? Do you seem to have things in common with them?

- What is the history of the organization? How old is it? Has it been growing, staying the same size over time, or getting smaller?

- What recent achievements has the organization made? What are the current projects you might end up working on?

Search for More Details

Do an internet search for the name of the organization. Make sure you look past the first page of results in order to determine what the media, financial analysts, and competitors are saying about it. When possible, seek out the organization's financial statements. If you can, compare statements over the past few years. Is revenue or profit declining over time? If so, can you figure out a good reason, or might the health of the organization be in question? If the organization is publicly traded, how has its stock price been moving relative to competitors or the market in general? You might also find interesting information from a Google News search.

Seek Out Other Perspectives

Use social media, blogs, and forums to learn what others think about the organization. Are reviews from past employees generally positive or negative? Do clients or customers seem satisfied with the products or services they receive? If you have a connection to someone who works at the organization, get their perspective as well. They may be able to help you put what you've learned from other sources into context.

Research Leading Up To The Interview

The impression of the organization that you developed through the initial research that we've described above should continue to develop as you are contacted to set up an interview. Is the process for scheduling casual (done by a chatty email or phone call) or is it more formal and bureaucratic (with a letter mailed to your home)? Do the people you talk to sound friendly? Do they sound like they know what they're doing or are they struggling to figure out how to schedule your interview?

Research During The Interview

When you arrive for the interview, you will have even more information to gather. What are people wearing? If you're invited back for a second interview, should you increase or decrease the formality of your clothing to match their look? Are people running from room to room hectically, walking at a normal pace, or meandering as if they have no need or desire to arrive at their destination? If you walk through a workspace to get to the interview room, is there much background noise? (Will you be able to get work done in a place where everyone whispers, where there are side conversations going on all the time, or where there are frequent loud disagreements?)

At some point during the interview, the interviewer will likely take a few minutes to give you more details about the job. This might include a description of the tasks or projects you will work on, who you will work with, or what the organization is like. Pay careful attention to what is said, and take notes on any key facts that you think you might forget before this potentially stressful day is over.

Here are some questions you may want to ask yourself as you learn more about the organization:

- Is your future manager someone you can learn from? Do you think they will be interested in facilitating your career development?

- Are you getting consistent impressions of the

company culture, or does the stated culture (as it appears on the company website or in the job ad) differ from what you're seeing and hearing from the interviewer?

- Do you think you would get along with your potential coworkers?

- If you have more than one interviewer, do they seem to get along, or at least respect each other?

- Does the work environment seem like a place where you might be productive?

- Would you have a chance to use the skills and knowledge that you hope to use?

- Is this job a good fit for your desired career path?

- Would you enjoy doing the work as you understand it?

- Do you think you would be able to meet or exceed the expectations and benchmarks for this job?

Keep in mind, one great way to find the answers to these questions is to ask.

Come Prepared With Questions

In order to ask questions of the interviewer that are

specific to your needs and that will give you useful information, think about what you want to know and how to ask about it ahead of time. Write your questions down in a prioritized list (from most important to least important) and take them with you to the interview. A prioritized list will come in handy if you don't have time to ask every question. You can always ask more questions in subsequent interviews, or after you've been offered the job but before you accept it. But it's nice to have answers to your most pressing questions so that you can decide whether or not you want to move on to the next phase of the job search.

Ask the Right Question of the Right Person

One of the most important things to learn before the interview is who will interview you. This doesn't mean you have to know where they went to school and the names of their pets (creepy!). It does mean that, at a minimum, you should know what they do at the company. Are you interviewing with people who you would manage, who would be your peers, who would be your boss, or with someone who is even higher up in the hierarchy? Are you interviewing with people you would work with on a daily basis, or are they just decision makers whom you wouldn't interact with? Who has hiring authority? You can usually find all of this out by asking the person who schedules your interview.

Having this information will help you to ask the right questions of the right people. Below, we walk you through a few examples of the types of questions you might ask and to whom you might ask these questions. The point is to ask questions of people who know the answers, not people who might have to guess. If someone can't give you the information you're looking for, ask them something else. For example, if you want to know how long employees typically stay at the company, you could ask anyone about the organization's turnover rate. But a representative from human resources is the person who is most likely to give you the most accurate answer. Other people could probably give you an estimate, but that estimate may be skewed toward those people's experiences. In other words, those answers will be based on smaller samples, like the employees in their team or in their department or the number of people who have left since they themselves were hired.

When talking to a human resources professional, ask questions about:

- Dress code (before the in-person interview)

- Responsibilities and duties

- Professional development and training opportunities

- Employee turnover rates

- Compensation and benefits (preferably not at the first interview, ideally you should try to wait until a job offer negotiation)

- Performance evaluation schedules and metrics

When interviewing with the hiring manager, ask questions about:

- Timeline for the hiring process

- Expectations for the new hire and traits sought

- That person's management style

- Requirements for or likelihood of advancement

- Duties and assignments

When talking to peers, ask questions about:

- Their impressions of management (but only if their boss isn't in the room!)

Anyone in the organization can provide you with details about:

- Organizational culture

- Their specific role in the organization

- Their career trajectory (e.g., how long they've been there, their promotion history)

- Their likes and dislikes about the organization

- Previous or upcoming changes in the organization (e.g., growth, restructuring)

- Industry-related questions and comparisons to competitor organizations

Do not ask about these topics—with anyone:

- Facts that can be found on the company's website or through a quick internet search

- Gossip about coworkers or the company

- One other note about your questions: they should be genuine. That is, you should honestly want to know the answers to these questions. Ideally, those answers will give you insight into whether you want to work in the job and for the organization.

Listen to Clues

Just as your questions will reflect what you want to know

about the job and the organization, the interviewer's questions will give you a sense of what topics are important to them. Their questions—especially behavioral and situational ones—can be good clues as to the types of situations and tasks that you will encounter on the job. If you're asked several questions about conflict—how you might handle conflict with customers, coworkers, and managers, for instance—you can expect to experience conflict in the job. The interviewer is giving you a hint that previous employees have experienced or created conflict in the past. If conflict makes you uncomfortable, you may want to seek clarification about this aspect of the position before accepting an offer.

Summary

- One of the two most important things to do during an interview is to figure out whether you want the job.

- Start your research of the organization early, and continue to evaluate the organization throughout your interactions with employees.

- Be ready to ask your own questions during the interview, and be sure that you're asking questions that are best answered by the person you're speaking with.

- Listen for hints about what you may encounter in the job by paying attention to the topics that the interviewer brings up.

CHAPTER 15

WHAT DO YOU KNOW ABOUT THIS COMPANY?

Question Type:

Industry and Company Specific

Question Analysis:

The interviewer will use this question to assess the research done by the candidate prior to the interview. If it is obvious that the candidate did little or no research on the company, it will raise red flags about how they might approach a challenging issue on the job. Tips 4, 5, 6, and 8 discuss excellent methods for researching the company. Great things to speak about here are the company's: core values, mission statement, industry, competition, product offerings, technology, geographic presence and competitive advantages.

What to Avoid:

The interview is not the time to bring up negative press about the company such as "I know they are being sued right now for a product malfunctioning." You should also avoid rehearsing information word-for-word from the company's website such as a paragraph long mission statement. This will not impress the interviewer. It would only show them that you are capable of memorizing. Instead, bullet point key information when you do your research and discuss it in a conversational tone.

Example Response:

While researching XYZ Company, I noted that your core values include: integrity, reliable, quality, and innovative. I believe strongly in each of these values and strive to make them characteristics of my own work. I know that the company is a market leader and currently holds the most patents in the consumer electronics industry. I also know that they have distribution in over 50 countries throughout the world.

Tell me about a time you took a leadership role. What was the outcome?

Question Type:

Behavioral

Question Analysis:

Leadership opportunities are not just part of management roles. Companies seek candidates who are strong leaders on projects and in other team settings. They also look for leadership qualities to assess the potential for a transition toward management positions in the future. The interviewer is looking for an example that has a favorable outcome as a direct result of your actions. A leadership example from your prior work experience is ideal but if you cannot come up with a strong example, an academic project or volunteer opportunity will suffice as well.

What to Avoid:

You should avoid examples that resulted in unfavorable outcomes or were largely uneventful. You should also not include too many unnecessary details. Sticking to the STAR method will help keep the example clear and concise.

Example Response:

S: In my last position as an account executive, our director of sales unexpectedly left the company three weeks before our annual strategic conference with over 100 of our top clients. Most people in our department started to panic because the director had such an instrumental role in facilitating the lineup of speakers and learning materials, but we did not have time to replace him.

T: The vice president of marketing asked me to step up and lead our department in coordinating with the speakers and finalizing all learning materials for the event.

A: The first thing I did was schedule a meeting with all five members of our team to map out what was accomplished and what still needed to be done. We created a timeline with the tasks we needed to complete and built in frequent update meetings to ensure we were all on the same page moving forward toward our goal. I also asked each member to come up with three new ideas to improve the learning experience for our clients. We then discussed them as a team and voted on the new ideas that would be incorporated into the event.

R: The conference was a success and I even had the opportunity to get up on stage and give a short presentation on one of the new ideas our team developed. Our clients had nothing but positive feedback about their experience and our vice president was very appreciative of my leadership.

What are three characteristics your co-workers would use to describe you?

Question Type:

Background and Personality

Question Analysis:

The interviewer will use this question to gauge whether the candidate's characteristics are a strong fit for the position. They also want to know if the candidate would fit in well with the company dynamics. An excellent way to come up with positive characteristics your co-workers would use to describe you is to think back to any positive feedback they provided while working closely together. Ideally, the characteristics you use in your response will align well with those sought after in the job description.

What to Avoid:

You should avoid generic responses such as "hard working" or "positive." You should also avoid traits that are not professional or specific to the job such as "outgoing" or "friendly."

Example Response:

My co-workers would describe me as dependable, organized, and innovative. When there is a tight deadline tied to my work, they know they can rely on me to complete it on time and have it done correct the first time. They would also point out that I frequently propose opportunities for improving existing processes and implementing new value-added measures.

Are you interviewing at other companies?

Question Type:

Ambition

Question Analysis:

The interviewer may ask this question for a number of reasons. Often, they want to know where a candidate is in the search process and whether the candidate is entertaining other offers. This knowledge may influence the timing of their offer as well as the terms of the compensation package. They might also use the question to validate the strength of the candidate by assessing their popularity with other potential employers. If you have already interviewed with competitors or have interviews coming up, it can be to your advantage to mention so but you should emphasize your interest and excitement in the current opportunity.

What to Avoid:

Assuming you are conducting a traditional search for a new job, you should typically avoid telling the interviewer you are not interviewing elsewhere. It can make you appear desperate for the position and the interviewer might wonder why you have not received other interviews. If you have applied at other companies but do not have any other outside interviews at the time, you can mention that you are in different phases of exploring opportunities with a few other companies. Perhaps you are not actively seeking other opportunities and the interviewer's company specifically sought you out for the job or you are pursuing this particular role for its unique fit for your career goals. In this case, speak succinctly about your reasoning for taking the interview. It goes without saying, but you should never lie to the interviewer. It is okay to be vague, but do not say you have other interviews if that is not true.

Where do you see yourself in five years?

Question Type:

Ambition

Question Analysis:

This question will help the interviewer gauge how committed the candidate is to the company. The question can catch some candidates off guard because they are so focused in on the position but have not given much thought to the future. The answer should be dependent on the position and industry. Some industries offer a lot of opportunities and growth without a definitive path to management. Other industries, such as public accounting, have a clear five or six-year path to a management position. It is important to conduct research on the position and emphasize your desire to embrace opportunities to grow within the company.

What to Avoid:

You should avoid responses that indicate complacency such as "I'll be happy if I am in this position five years from now." Interviewers typically look for candidates to express an eagerness to grow and advance within the company. You should also avoid unrealistic and smug responses such as "CEO of the company" or "I plan to have your job."

Example Response:

One of the main reasons I applied for this position was for the chance to work at a company that offers so many growth opportunities to its employees. Over the next five years I see myself taking advantage of those opportunities by taking on additional responsibilities as an individual contributor and as part of a team. As I establish credibility and continue to grow over the next five years, I see myself moving into a management or leadership position within the finance department.

Why do you want to work here?

Question Type:

Ambition

Question Analysis:

The interviewer will use this question to ensure the candidate is interested in the position for the right reasons and has done some homework on the company. Your answer should include specifics about the company that show a strong level of interest and enthusiasm.

What to Avoid:

You should avoid responses that are overly generic such as "I want to work here because this is an excellent company." The interviewer will view this response as an indication that did not do sufficient research on the position or company. You should also avoid misinformed responses. Be sure to have your facts straight about the company and position and avoid bringing up items you are not sure about.

Example Response:

I first became interested in XYZ Company when I saw Forbes Magazine list it as a top 100 company to work for in the world. I did further research and found that it is known for fostering a collaborative and innovative culture. This type of work setting is exactly what I am looking for and I feel that my personality and aspirations would be a perfect fit. I am also very excited about the potential opportunity to work on the supply chain team to leverage my prior experience with SAP while supporting procurement teams all over the world.

Why did you choose to go into this profession?

Question Type:

Ambition

Question Analysis:

The interviewer will use this question to find out if the candidate researched the profession and orchestrated a calculated plan or if it was more random chance that led them into the profession. Even if there were random variables that lead you down your career path, your answer should focus on the purposeful decisions you made to move forward in your profession as well as the experience that affirmed that decision. It will tell the interviewer you understand the industry and have a vested interest in sticking around long-term. It will also show that you are methodical when making significant decisions.

What to Avoid:

You should avoid placing too much emphasis on random events that factored into your career path. If there were unexpected events that lead you down your path, you can touch on them but emphasize how your research or experience affirmed your decision.

Example Response:

I had always wanted to pursue a career in technology and wanted to ensure that I went into a field that had diverse opportunities and was on the cutting edge of innovation. After speaking with a few professors and career advisors my freshman year of college, I was confident that I wanted to become a web developer. I then made it my mission to connect with web developers in the area to get a better sense of their day-to-day work. That opened the door for an internship and eventual first job after college. My experience as a web developer has affirmed my decision to go into the profession. Looking back on my decision, I would not change a thing.

Describe your ideal boss.

Question Type:

Background and Personality

Question Analysis:

Interviewers will usually ask this question to get a sense of the type of leadership style the candidate works best under. The answer will provide them with a better understanding of the candidate's work style. In your response, you should demonstrate that you have no problem working independently but also have an appreciation and respect for authority. You should try to focus your answer in on characteristics that are conducive to the company's values and culture.

What to Avoid:

Some interviewers use this question as a test to see whether the candidate will criticize a former boss. You should avoid responses that imply you had a negative relationship with a prior boss. The interviewer may take the criticism of a former boss as a sign that you are difficult to manage.

Example Response:

I've been fortunate to work for a couple excellent bosses

in the past. To me, an ideal boss leads by example and helps to create shared vision for the team. Their own actions have a large impact on team morale and can be an inspiration to those around them. An ideal boss trusts their employees to get the job done but possesses excellent communication skills when their input is needed. Finally, an ideal boss maintains a positive outlook and focuses on solutions instead of looking for blame when something goes wrong.

Tell me about a time you failed. What did you learn?

Question Type:

Behavioral

Question Analysis:

Since the purpose of the interview is to leave a highly positive impression, talking about failure can be difficult for most candidates. The interviewer will ask this question because they want to know that the candidate can acknowledge and learn from failure. Failure can be ambiguous, so it can be beneficial to define what failure means to you before providing an example. In your example, you should discuss why you failed and how you learned from it.

What to Avoid:

You should avoid an underwhelming example such as "I was only rated a four out of five on my employee evaluation." The interviewer knows that everyone fails occasionally so you should discuss a genuine example. With that said, you should not discuss any examples that would scare the interviewer such as "I fell for a financial phishing scam and cost our company a million dollars." You should avoid discussing a substantial lapse in judgement or a sloppy error.

Example Response:

S: Most people only think of failure as events with significant consequences, but I consider myself to have failed each time I do not meet my goals and expectations. The key for me is to recognize even the smallest of failures so that I can learn from them and make adjustments. In my current role as a cost accountant, I am in charge of producing our annual budget for our largest production plant.

T: My first year creating the budget, I met with the managers at the plant to discuss the material, labor, and overhead projections for the upcoming fiscal year. The production plan seemed straight forward for the year, which lead to my confidence in compiling the budget. However, the managers forgot to mention a pending capital expenditure project and I failed to review the project management system to identify it.

A: The project ended up going through in the current year and as a result, the actual depreciation expense for the year was 20% higher than in my budget. In my explanation of the variance, I was honest about the fact that I neglected to reference the project management system to substantiate the budget inputs for new projects.

R: I quickly learned that when creating forecasts and budgets, validating information and data is just as important as collecting it. Going forward, I developed a systematic approach to substantiate all information and assumptions in my budgets. In each of the prior three years, my budget to actual variances have been the lowest in our whole department.

What is a significant challenge facing the profession (accounting, finance, nursing, engineering, etc.) today?

Question Type:

Industry and Company Specific

Question Analysis:

The interviewer will use this question to assess the candidate's awareness of the current hot topics in the profession. They want to see that the candidate has not only followed news and trends in the profession but also considered the ramifications of some of the challenges it faces. Your answer should demonstrate that you have an inherent interest in the profession and have thought through how recent events or trends could disrupt it.

What to Avoid:

You should try to avoid answers that do not discuss why the challenges are specific to the profession such as "outsourcing is eliminating jobs." Your answer should explain the issue and then discuss why it is particularly challenging to your profession.

Example response (accounting profession):

Cloud accounting programs and applications have had a significant impact on the profession. My opinion is that they can be both a challenge and an opportunity. The cloud technology today has made it much easier for those who do not necessarily have accounting or bookkeeping experience to book entries and access financial reporting. The opportunity is that the technology has enabled accountants and financial analysts to focus less on the data entry and more on the reporting and decision making. The challenge is that many businesses are relying too heavily on software and technology and not utilizing the skills of a qualified accountant. This can save them resources in the short-term but can also increase the risk of costly reporting or regulatory errors.

CHAPTER 16

PROFESSIONAL DEVELOPMENT AND TRAINING

A focus on this during the recruiting process is important (more so than ever before) and needs to be to be dealt with in detail – starting off when reading the application documents. Questions about the reasons behind previous or planned professional training reveal much about the candidate's character, career goals and his ability to continually develop professional skills. Direct your questions with an eye on your job-requirements, the candidate's own expectations and what your company can offer in terms of further training in the long-term.

Our company offers the following training courses…. Which of those would be the most interesting for you?

How well does the candidate put eventual deficits into relation to the requirements of your job and how honestly and intelligently does he answer?

In which two or three areas would you need to develop

your skills to be able to excel in our job?

This concrete question should lead to a substantive response. It's a fair question that doesn't put too much pressure on the candidate. Out of the answer you should be able to recognize the level of motivation for further training, how self-critical the candidate is and if he has really understood the job requirements.

Which skills and qualifications would you like to improve?

An indirect way to find out more about weaknesses, skill gaps, motivation to learn and determination. The answer shows how objectively, self-critically the candidate assesses himself, how cleverly he matches his skills and professional qualifications with your vacancy and whether he has even thought about how to improve eventual deficiencies.

When it comes to asking about weaknesses or optimization possibilities, it is good to sometimes ask less directly and in a softer, watered-down way without negative undertones. This increases the chance of getting honest answers and more information about the candidate and whether he can meet the requirements of the vacant position.

How do you keep up to date with professional and specialist developments?

The question provides information on specific activities, the degree and the level of interest in further education and the latest developments in the candidate's subject area. In addition, it also says a lot about general motivation, personality and character.

What are your main criteria for choosing training or further education?

Here you get to know how the candidate assesses himself. Are his answers general or specific, do they evidence true interest in the subject? Interesting is to see if the candidate refers to your job requirement and responsibilities when answering.

Which new trends and developments in your field of expertise do you think are particularly important?

The answer reveals the level of interest for the candidate's area of expertise and provides information about his qualifications as a whole. Does the candidate pro-actively think about the future of his field or is he somewhat passive?

Presuming you get the job, in which areas would you take further training?

If the candidate manages to give a concrete answer it shows that he has thoroughly looked into the details of the job-description, the main requirements, the priorities he will have to set and critically compared them with his current level of expertise or know-how.

From which training courses in the past did you develop your set of skills the most?

The answer should help you find out whether the candidate's ideas and priorities match your corporate Human Resources development concept. A clear-cut answer shows a realistic self-assessment and reveals the candidate's present level of know-how. Are skills named and brought across convincingly, is there evidence that the candidate planned his career and developed it thoughtfully? Take note to what extent the skills match the requirements of your vacancy.

What major changes and challenges in your field of expertise will we be seeing in the coming years?

The answer shows the candidate's level of knowledge and competence in his professional area. Is he able to synthesize relevant information and express his point of view, where do his priorities lie? If he works in a fast-moving environment - and wishes to continue doing so –

interest in further training and the ability to adapt are a must.

What professional literature have you read recently?

The response reveals whether the candidate reads at all, what topics he's interested in, what priority he gives further training and if he's willing to learn in his own time. Again, it is interesting to see whether his areas of interest match the requirements of your vacancy.

Supposing we would offer you a training course, what would interest you most?

The answer is interesting, for similar reasons as the previous one. However here we see even more clearly whether the candidate's interests are aligned to the specifications of the vacant job, which specialized extensive training he chooses and in which area there are know-how deficits.

What would interest you the most in personality training?

A tricky question which one should be careful about asking; but which will certainly reveal which areas of his personality he would like to develop. Besides the topics, the way (diplomatic, differentiated, clever etc.) the candidate answers reveals a lot about his they say otherwise.

Answers To 50 Tough Job Interview Questions

Tough questions asked during job interviews are more than likely asked to check if you can think on your feet than make you feel jittery and nervous. If you remember this trick, you will cease to be overwhelmed by the fear of answering tough questions.

Furthermore, I have asked several professionals who conduct job interviews as a requirement for their daily jobs. They include a Retail Managers, University Professors, Recruiters, Senior Directors, Consultants, and multiple CEOs. Furthermore, I have also included questions from many current working employees and asked them what has been the toughest interview question they have had and what questions did they think was the deciding factor in their current position. A holistic approach was utilized in crafting these tough interview questions to ensure quality and transparency in their nature.

Once again, it is important to know that you do not memorize these answers word by word. However, familiarize yourself with these answers and practice. Your preparation and understanding of certain common yet tough questions can be the difference between landing your dream job or just being another applicant.

What is your biggest weakness and how have you overcome it? - I am a fairly impatient person. If things do not go perfectly when I delegate work, then it is possible for me to do the work myself. However, I ensure I do a lot of prep work so that the person to whom I delegate the work rarely falls below my expectations.

Are you here to take my position? – Yes, very much. I hope to take over your position in about 4-5 years by which time you will become the CEO and you will need a trusted person in your old job.

I can see you have had plenty of jobs up until now. Are you using this job to see it fits you or are you convinced that it's the right one for you? I intend to use the cumulative skills to help in the growth of this company as well.

How come you did not try to jump ship despite knowing that your previous company was in doldrums? – I was working too hard at my job to notice small changes that were reflective of bigger things to come. And, moreover, with mergers happening all over in the industry, I cannot keep running away from potential layoffs. At least, I know I have given my best.

There is one instance in your previous history that shows you have not got promoted despite working at the place for over 5 years. Why is that? – Today, the company you are talking about is doing very well. However, when I was working there, layoffs were common and holding onto the job was a huge achievement. Still, the skills and knowledge that I picked up from that place are unparalleled and the experience was wonderful despite the glaring absence of a promotion.

How come you were fired more than once from your previous jobs? – Yes, I have been laid off twice and I was shocked both times. However, after the initial disappointment, I managed to secure better-paying and better profile jobs in both the cases.

Suppose you owned a company that was manufacturing a product, which was not relevant in the market anymore, what would you do? – I would search the globe for a new market while I encourage my engineers to tweak or change the product to suit the new demands of the existing market.

You are 40-plus now. Why do you want to start at

the entry level? – It is a commonly accepted philosophy that sometimes we may have to move a step back to advance forward. And that is what I am doing. The industry I worked for until now is quite different from this and it makes a lot of sense to work my way up from the bottom to ensure that I have a total understanding of the job and can give my best to it.

Why did you not join the bank where you did a short-term internship? Did your performance during the internship not meet their expectations? – Yes, I did complete an internship at the bank mentioned and it was a highly successful one. I have recommendation letters that prove how well the people appreciated my performance. However, when I completed my course, the bank was laying off many employees and hiring was frozen. Today, I believe that this seemingly unlucky break was actually a lucky one since I was compelled to look elsewhere and that's what brought me to this job interview.

While we love diversity in our company, for this particular position, which involves interacting with Southeast Asian countries, however, we are keen on recruiting Asian males. – How would you as a white female, deal with this type of diversity if you were to get hired? – I have learned a great deal with the Asian culture and many of my friends are that of Asian descent. I love working with many diverse people and I believe my skills and background would translate well with working with this particular group of people, as well as, being successful in this particular position.

Why did you have to take such a long break from work? Why do you want to get back to work now? – I quit my job earlier for the sake of my newborn baby. My spouse was on a 24/7 job and one of us had to sacrifice time for our child and I chose to. Now, that my child is old enough to manage independently, I am happy to get back to work as I really miss the work. (It is important to tell the truth and not an excuse. Just be frank, while also being appropriate while answering the question. For example, saying you had personal or a family tragedy for instance, is completely fine to say. Remember to not ramble about personal stories. Keep it succinct and professional.

OR

I had family and health emergencies I needed to tend to before I wanted to start work again. By taking care of those I love first, I can then focus on my career because my family has provided so much for me.

We are an ethnic company and all our customers are more comfortable with ethnic people rather than people like you. Hence, I am hesitating to hire you. – As a writer, the one qualification that is as important as my writing skills is to have empathy. If you were to look beyond my skin color, you would see my high level of experience and qualifications and would appreciate that your company and your customers would gain from their interaction with me.

Suppose you want to hire a woman for a job in your team and your boss wants a man in that position. What would you do? – I would hire both on a two-week trial basis as freelancers and make the choice after experimenting with both.

How would you handle a situation in which the person you are working with takes all credit? – I would first publicly credit her own ideas as this will kind of make her obliged to return the favor. Otherwise, we could arrange to present each of our ideas separately to the boss. I could openly discuss my feelings of resentment and arrive at an amicable solution.

How many hours can you put in each week? – I usually work long hours. During the additional time I work, I try and see if there are some improvements I can make for my clients. When customers see my work, they are left with no doubt that it is my company that has done their work.

Do you think it is good for a company to have only A players on its payroll? – No, I believe it is better to have a balanced set of A and B players on the payroll. This is because it is highly likely that too many A players can create undue and harmful friction leading to more losses than gains for the company. Moreover, while A players run the customer interface, the B players can focus on hammering out the ops details which are critical to the success of any company.

Are you a "managing up" person or a "managing down" person? – I personally believe that if I do not know how to do the former, I can never be successful with the latter. I am flexible can manage both ways.

Would you get permission from your boss to try out something new or would you like to be free from such red-tape measures? – To me, it's always important to ask my supervisor if it's okay to venture out new assignments or tasks that would help the company perform better. After some time have past, maybe 6 months, and building good rapport with my supervisor, I would only try out something new if I were fully confident if it would impact the company in a positive direction.

Give us an example of how you managed a tricky situation at one of your previous jobs – When my first boss hired me, he had already planned to retire within a few days after he hired me. He simply passed on all his assignments to me. I completed the assignments and left them on his desk a week prior his resignation. I also forwarded the same completed assignments to the new boss to ensure a smooth transition to my new supervisor. This kept both the boss and the other people content.

What do you think is more important for success in the workplace; skill or luck? – I think it is normal for people to say that skill is more important than luck for success. However, I have always believed that both aspects play an important role in the success of an individual. You need luck for good opportunities to come along and you need the skill to grab and hold onto some of those opportunities. Furthermore, I believe luck arises when skill, practice, and perseverance have occurred.

At what age do you think you will reach a peak in your performance? – As I come from a family of mentally, physically and emotionally healthy people, I have never thought of "peaking" at any point. However, I do understand that advancing age can give you the maturity to step down at a time when someone is ready to take over from you.

When do you think it is right to break a confidence? – I will not hesitate to break the confidence of a friend or colleague if he or she has confided in me that he/she has done something illegal.

Do you believe you are a leader? – Yes, undoubtedly. I am a great listener but can talk sense into people as well. I love following big ideas but also know when to be practical and sensible.

What do you see as a disadvantage in the position you have applied for? – I believe that collaborating with people from different time zones and geographical zones is going to be a challenge. However, modern-day collaborative tools such as video conferencing, faxes, emails, etc. will easily help me overcome these challenges.

Can you give an example of an unpopular decision you took? – At one workplace, I had a boss who managed four different offices and was really short on time. He wanted me to play the role of a quasi-boss during his absence. I did not agree to this as I already knew the fate of several quasi-bosses that he had appointed unofficially with neither a new formal contract nor an official announcement.

Despite knowing that this would anger him, I flatly refused, saying that I would take on the role only if he made an official announcement and made suitable changes in my contract. It did make my life more difficult than before at that office, but I am glad that I chose to be upfront and honest with my boss rather than agree to present an ingratiating attitude.

personality.

CONCLUSION

Now you should start preparing for interviews. Since most recruiters use a similar format for their interviews, we'll focus on the three most common types of questions: opening questions, fit questions, and case questions.

Let's start with opening questions. The most common question in any job interview is: "Can you tell me about yourself?" This is the recruiter's way of seeing if you can communicate relevant information about yourself. Your response will set the tone for the rest of the interview. If you nail it, you'll start with a strong first impression. The recruiter will be rooting for you throughout the rest of the interview. If you bomb it, the recruiter may rule you out before you get to the next question.

My favorite way to answer this question to use a technique called the P-E-N framework. This framework can be extremely powerful for organizing your answers in clear, compelling ways. The P-E-N framework can be used to answer a variety of opening questions, including the following:

- Can you tell me about yourself?

- Will you walk me through your resume?

- Can you tell me why you're interested in this job?

- Why should I hire you?

With strong answers to these questions, you'll distinguish yourself from other candidates who want the same jobs you want. You should keep practicing and refining your answers to these questions until you have responses that will absolutely dazzle recruiters.

All the best!

Lightning Source UK Ltd.
Milton Keynes UK
UKHW020818210521
384121UK00009B/234